Is Mormonism Christian?

Is Mormonism Christian?

An Examination of Mormon Doctrine as Compared with Orthodox Christianity

by

GORDON H. FRASER

MOODY PRESS
CHICAGO

REVISED EDITION
1965

Printed in the United States of America

CONTENTS

INTRODUCTION

WHAT DO WE MEAN by *Christian?*

Ask the average man on the street and he will tell you, "Anyone is a Christian who is not a Jew or an atheist."

The Mormons have striven for years to gain recognition as a Christian body. Until within a decade or so, their claim has been denied by even the more liberal groups of professing Christians. Lately, however, with a general lowering of Christian standards of thought, and with a remarkable build-up in the public press and on the radio, the Mormons have achieved their goal in the thinking of the general public.

But are the Mormons Christians?

If the term covers all who use the name of Christ in their titles or in their teaching, we would have to allow the Mormons their claim; but we would have to include with them the Jehovah's Witnesses, Christian Scientists, and most of the other metaphysical cults, as well as Unitarians, Universalists, Bahaists, and a host of so-called liberal adherents to the various Christian denominations which, originally, were completely orthodox.

All of these refer freely to Jesus Christ and use quotations from the Bible to support their views but, these, along with the Mormons, deny what we consider to be the indispensable tenets of true, orthodox, historic Christianity.

In the present study we shall examine the doctrines of Mormonism against the background of the following Biblical doctrines—

1. That the Godhead is triune.
2. That God the Father, God the Son, and God the Holy Spirit are coequal and coeternal.
3. That Jesus Christ is the eternal Son of God, and was manifested in the flesh to accomplish redemption by His sacrificial death on Calvary.
4. That man is a sinner both by nature and by practice.
5. That man may become a child of God only by availing himself of the work of redemption as provided by the death of Christ.
6. That salvation is eternal and is obtained only as a gift by the grace of God, apart from self-effort.
7. That good works are the product of the regener-

ated life and are not a means of acquiring or perpetuating salvation.

8. That salvation is available to "whosoever will," regardless of the degree to which the sinner has descended in his departure from righteousness.
9. That the Bible is the inerrant Word of God.
10. That it was written by men inspired by the Holy Spirit of God and that it contains all that is necessary for us to know concerning: the Person and work of Deity; the origin, nature and destiny of man; the nature and consequences of sin; the means of progress in the spiritual life of the believer; the conduct of Christians in their mutual fellowships as a witnessing Church.

* * *

Before proceeding with our study we must pause to explain that there are six distinct religious bodies that revolve within the orbit of the *Book of Mormon,* and the prophetic leadership of Joseph Smith. For the information of our readers these groups are designated as follows:

1. The Church of Jesus Christ of Latter-day Saints, with headquarters in Salt Lake City, Utah. These are known as the "Brighamite" Mormons since they claim Brigham Young as the authorized successor to Joseph Smith.

2. The Reorganized Church of Jesus Christ of Latter-day Saints with headquarters in Independence, Missouri. This group, second in numerical strength, is known as the "Josephite" Church since it insists that the succession to the prophetic office must descend in the direct lineage of Joseph Smith. This group consists of those who refused the leadership of Brigham Young and rallied to the support of Emma Smith, the first wife of Joseph the Prophet.
3. The Church of Christ, Temple Lot "Hedrickite," with headquarters in Independence, Missouri. This group, though small, is quite vigorous and claims to be the only true church by reason of the fact that it is in possession of the lot designated by Joseph Smith in 1831 as the site of the Temple of Zion. It displays with pride the stone markers inscribed and placed by Joseph Smith as the marker stones of the temple site.
4. The Church of Jesus Christ, "Bickertonite." This group was joined and supported by Sidney Rigdon, ex-Baptist, ex-Campbellite who became Joseph Smith's theologian in the early days of Mormonism. Rigdon was opposed to the polygamous ideas of Joseph Smith and was expelled from the church in Nauvoo, Illinois, for insubordination. A final act of rebellion was said to be his

refusal to give his daughter, Nancy, to Smith as a plural wife.

5. The Church of Jesus Christ, "Cutlerite," followed Alpheus Cutler who claimed a vision which assured him that he was to be the successor to Joseph Smith. This group had a following in Northern Iowa and Wisconsin. It is now quite insignificant.
6. The Church of Jesus Christ of Latter-day Saints, "Strangite," followed the leadership of James J. Strang, a latecomer to the ranks of Mormonism in Nauvoo. Strang was a dominant personality who claimed to be the successor to the prophet on the strength both of seeing visions and receiving a letter from Smith dated just ten days prior to the murder of Smith. Strang was ousted from the church by the Brigham Young faction and the letter repudiated, although there is strong evidence that the letter did exist. Strang fostered polygamy and was in process of building a strong organization in Northern Michigan. He set himself up as king, but his kingdom died and his followers scattered when Strang was shot from ambush by some of his outraged followers. The Strangites are now almost extinct.

In fairness it must be said that all of these groups, except the Brighamites and the Strangites, repudiated polygamy and have retreated from the extreme Adam-God idea of the Brighamites, and with some reservations, from the doctrine of baptism for the dead. If it were not for their adherence to the *Book of Mormon* as the Word of God and their acknowledgment of the prophetic office of Joseph Smith, they would pass as Christian churches if not scrutinized too closely.

We have no questions as to the moral uprightness of these groups which did not follow Strang or Brigham Young. We do question their methods of evading the implications of Mormonism. As long as these groups retain Joseph Smith as their prophet and his writings as the inspired Word of God, they cannot escape being involved in the false doctrines that were stated in his writings and in his discourses.

It is with these unbiblical doctrines, as brought to full flower by the Salt Lake Church, that we are concerned in this study.

If some arrow glances off the main target and inflicts a wound in any of the other groups, it is because they deliberately stand exposed to its flight.

* * *

Our sole purpose in this study is to alert marginal or uninformed Christians to the true character of the Mormon doctrines. Additions to the Mormon Church (and these are increasing rapidly) come almost invariably from the ranks of established Christian groups, and almost always from those who are uncertain concerning the doctrine of salvation and other Biblical truths.

The Mormon missionaries are well trained in their methods, and nominal Christians are an easy prey to their arguments. We have yet to see, however, an intelligent, born-again person, who knows the Bible and its doctrines, succumb to Mormonism.

The Mormon missionaries who come to your door will be well-mannered attractive young people. They will introduce themselves as "Christian missionaries" or will use some other innocuous term. One team, which had recently returned from Honduras, announced themselves as members of the Central American Mission. Another team encountered recently merely asked: "Could we step in and have a Christian word with you?" They will avoid identifying themselves as Mormons or Latter-day Saints until after they have gained an audience.

These young missionaries are given very careful training both in the fine points of good sales approach and in the best methods of appealing to members of the various churches. It is part of their training to attend services of the various churches so as to be informed on matters of phraseology and doctrine.

We should insist that such visitors identify themselves. If they prove to be Latter-day Saints or Mormons, the only safe procedure is to deny them entrance to the home. This is in keeping with the instruction given by John the apostle to "the elect lady."

> If there come any unto you, and bring not this doctrine [of Christ], receive him not into your house, neither bid him God speed: for he that biddeth him God speed is partaker of his evil deeds (II John 10, 11).

CHAPTER ONE

MORMONS AND THE BIBLE

IN ORDER TO EVALUATE the teachings of Mormonism it is necessary to capture the thinking of the Mormons: (1) on their concept of the inspiration of the Bible; and (2) the values placed by them on their own writings.

Two items in the doctrinal statement of the Mormons are involved in this discussion. The first, Article 8, of the *Articles of Faith,* which is the official published doctrinal statement of the Mormon Church, says:

> We believe the Bible to be the Word of God, as far as it is translated correctly; we also believe the *Book of Mormon* to be the Word of God.

The second, Article 9, states:

> We believe all that God has revealed, all that he does now reveal, and we believe that he will reveal

many great and important things pertaining to the Kingdom of God.

The Mormons believe in a progressive revelation, as is indicated by their acceptance of the *Book of Mormon* as the Word of God in Article 8, and in the latitude they allow themselves for later "revelations" in Article 9. (These doctrinal statements were not formulated or published until after the writings of Joseph Smith were completed, probably in 1843.) Smith's writings expanded as the need arose for new "scriptures" to substantiate the evolution of his theology. As an example of this we can observe that the evolution of Smith's writings developed in direct ratio to his deteriorating concept of God.

For the benefit of our readers who are not familiar with the writings of Joseph Smith, which are accepted by the Mormons as being equal to the Bible in their inspiration, we give the following outline. The works listed are given in the order in which they were produced although they were not given to the public in this order:

1. The *Book of Mormon,* 1830.

2. The *Covenants and Commandments,* later the *Doctrines and Covenants,* "revelations" given to Joseph Smith, 1830-1843.

3. The *Inspired Version* of the Bible, 1832 (?), first published by the Reorganized Church in 1866.

4. The *Pearl of Great Price,* including the "Book of Moses," "Book of Abraham," and "a choice selection from the revelations, translations and narrations of Joseph Smith," 1833-1835. First printed in 1851.

5. The *King Follett Discourse.* A funeral discourse delivered in 1844.

In the *Book of Mormon* the concept of God does not differ greatly from that in the Bible, although no discernment is exercised in the proper usage of the several Biblical names of God. In the *Inspired Version* of the Bible, which came next in Smith's writings, and in the "Book of Moses" of the *Pearl of Great Price,* which are identical, God had become anthropomorphic. This is in keeping with Paul's statement in Romans 1:23 regarding the deterioration of the gentile worship: "They changed the glory of the uncorruptible God into an image made like to corruptible man."

In the "Book of Abraham," which follows the "Book of Moses" in the *Pearl of Great Price,* a definite polytheism had developed. God had become one of a number of gods.

In the *Doctrines and Covenants* which accumulated over a period of twelve years, God was presented as having a body of flesh and bones.[1]

[1] *Doctrines and Covenants,* 130:22.

In the *King Follett Discourse,* which was presented during the closing year of Smith's life, God is depicted as "once as we are now, and is an exalted man."[2] These heretical teachings will be more fully developed in a later chapter.

* * *

A brief outline of the several volumes which constitute the Mormon scriptures is in order. More than a brief summary would be impossible in a volume of this size.

The *Book of Mormon* came first. It was supposedly translated from golden plates which Smith located, under the direction of the Angel Moroni, in a chest hidden on a hillside close to the Smith farm near Palmyra, New York.

These plates were represented as being inscribed in "reformed Egyptian" and contained the record of several migrations to the American continent in Old Testament times. The development of these migrations into civilizations, and their history until the fifth century A.D., constitute the main theme of the book.

Mormon teachers insist that the American Indians were descended from these migrants, who were Jews who left Jerusalem in 600 B.C., and came to America via the Pacific. Hence, according to the

[2] *King Follett Discourse*, p. 8.

Mormons, the Indians are Semites and constitute the lost tribes of Israel.[3]

The book tells of the coming of the resurrected Christ to America where He preached to the inhabitants which resulted in the formation of a Christian church in America in the first century A.D. This church disappeared during the fourth century A.D.

The translation of the plates was effected by means of a pair of spectacles found with the golden plates, called by Smith the Urim and Thummim. There are many conflicting stories about the method of translation. One of Smith's versions is that, when the Urim and Thummim were placed over the "reformed Egyptian" characters, they appeared to him in English.

It is doubtful if Smith had anything but a nebulous idea that the *Book of Mormon* would ever become the basis of a religion. His first thought evidently was one of writing a novel for profit.

During the writing of the book, Smith and his scribe, Oliver Cowdry, apparently conceived the idea of starting a new church and by the time of the pub-

[3] The Mormons are faced with the embarrassing fact that they have another version of the origin of the inhabitants of the Americas. This second version is as "authentic" as the *Book of Mormon* version since it was revealed by Joseph Smith on May 19, 1838, at Spring Hill, Missouri, and is recorded in *Doctrines and Covenants,* sections 116-117. Talmage defends this version in his *Articles of Faith,* p. 474. On pp. 283-284 of the same book, Talmage defends the *Book of Mormon* version.

lication of the book, Cowdry and Smith claimed to have received visions and each baptized and ordained the other, supposedly upon the instructions of John the Baptist:

> who visited us upon this occasion and conferred this [Aaronic] priesthood upon us . . . and that he acted under the direction of Peter, James and John, who held the keys of the Priesthood of Melchizedek, which priesthood . . . would in due time be conferred upon us, and that I should be called the first Elder of the church, and he [Oliver Cowdry] the second. It was on the fifteenth day of May, 1829, that we were ordained under the hand of this messenger and baptized.[4]

Several years later, when Cowdry was making a defense after having been expelled from the Church, he made a very enlightening remark regarding the identity of the messenger who had been identified as John the Baptist. Cowdry stated:

> I received baptism by the direction of the Angel of God, whose voice, as it has since struck me, did most mysteriously resemble the voice of Elder Sidney Rigdon.[5]

[4] Extract from the "History of Joseph Smith" as recorded in the *Pearl of Great Price,* pp. 98-99.

[5] Oliver Cowdry, *Defense.* (Sidney Rigdon was soon to become Joseph Smith's theologian if indeed he was not already in touch with Smith.)

Witnesses to the veracity of the "divinely revealed work" were soon forthcoming from the accumulating members of the new church. Three witnesses, Oliver Cowdry, David Whitmer, and Martin Harris signed their names to a statement, the gist of which follows:

> That we . . . have seen the plates . . . and we also know that they have been translated by the gift and power of God . . . and we also testify that we have seen the engravings which are upon the plates . . . and we declare with words of soberness, than an Angel of God came down from heaven, and he brought and laid before our eyes that we beheld and saw the plates and the engravings thereon . . .[6]

Smith quickly became dissatisfied with this testimony of the three since all three gave conflicting stories as to the event. Before the book could go to press, eight additional witnesses were secured who declared that they had seen and hefted the plates.

In the first edition of the *Book of Mormon,* this statement of the eight witnesses declares that Joseph Smith, Jr., was "author and proprietor of this work." This statement also appeared on the title page of the first edition.

The subsequent editions have the eight witnesses saying that Smith was "translator" of the book. The

[6] Preface to the *Book of Mormon.*

title page is also changed. I. W. Riley remarks that "the name of author and proprietor of the *Book of Mormon* was inadvertently assumed and quickly discarded."[7]

This transition from "author" to "translator" was a development. The "revelation" authorizing Smith's new title came several weeks after the publication of the *Book of Mormon*. The *Book of Commandments*, later called *Doctrines and Covenants*, records this revelation, under the date of April 6, 1830, as follows: "Thou shalt be called a seer, a translator, a prophet, an apostle of Jesus Christ."[8] Mormons are quite vehement in insisting that Smith was the translator and not the author of the *Book of Mormon*.

Of the first three witnesses, Cowdry, who received the first endowment jointly with Joseph Smith, was expelled from the Church for a host of misdoings, including disorderly conduct and counterfeiting. Previously, while still within the Church, he had been disciplined for adultery.

Martin Harris, who had been one of Smith's earliest supporters and had financed the first edition of the *Book of Mormon*, admitted later that he had seen the plates "by the eye of faith."

Harris was always more or less of a problem to Smith because of his loose talk. Finally he was ex-

[7] I. Woodbridge Riley, *The Founder of Mormonism*, p. 177.
[8] *Doctrines and Covenants*, 21:1.

pelled as an apostate after he had rallied to the support of a young "seeress" who used a black stone to see into the future.[9] In his later years, Harris rejoined the Mormons and was brought by the Brighamites to Utah. He proved, however, to be more of a problem than a trophy and little more was heard of him, although he was given suitable honors at his death.

David Whitmer had been expelled from the Church, together with Martin Harris and Cowdry in the episode of the young seeress, but was reinstated and sent west with Cowdry on business for the Church. By 1837, just seven years after the book was printed, all of the second group of witnesses, except Joseph's father and brothers, had either been expelled from the Church as apostates or had left of their own accord.

Thus all three of the first and five of the second group of witnesses were later repudiated by Smith.

When we consider the fact that Smith claimed that these witnesses were all "commanded by the Lord"[10] to be witnesses we cannot help but question the omniscience of Smith's god.

* * *

In 1830 Joseph realized that the Bible, as it was, and the *Book of Mormon* were not sufficient as a

[9] Fawn McKay Brodie, *No Man Knows My History*, p. 205.
[10] Preface to the *Book of Mormon*.

basis for his expanding theology. This was especially true in the matter of his evolving priesthood ideas. He now started the *Inspired Version* of the Bible. One of his apologists states:

> The New Testament scriptures are the Word of God as far as translated correctly. Joseph Smith undertook a revision of the scripture in the only way possible—by revelation.[11]

This same writer states in commenting on the text of Scripture:

> In general, it is well not to use a single passage of scripture in proof of a point, *unless it is confirmed by modern revelation*. If a single quotation is *confirmed by modern revelation,* we may be sure of its interpretation. . . . "No man has seen God at any time" (John 1:18) is not in harmony with other scriptures. In such cases, either the text has not come down correctly to the present or it has been incorrectly translated.[12]

By "modern revelation" Baker means the "revelations" given to Joseph Smith. No one but Smith was qualified to receive revelations.

In the *Inspired Version,* Smith mounts upon the framework of the King James Version a great deal of matter that is completely non-Biblical and has no

[11] James L. Barker, *The Divine Church,* p. 9.
[12] *Ibid.*

justification except to document his doctrines. Several hundreds of verses are added to Genesis and many others are changed to suit Smith's ideas.

The Creation story and the lives of Adam and his family are grossly distorted and much imaginative material is added. The life of Enoch is expanded by several chapters of extraneous material intended by Smith and Rigdon to give weight to the communistic "Order of Enoch" which was soon abandoned. The story of Melchizedek is much enlarged to provide "scriptural" background for the Mormon priesthood ideas. The corresponding portion in the Epistle to the Hebrews is altered to serve this purpose.

Anyone reading Mormon tracts or expository works should be careful to check the supposed Bible references. The expression "as one of the old prophets has written" is usually followed by a quotation from a purely Mormon scripture. One should especially check any supposed quotations from the Bible. The Mormons may choose to quote from the King James Version, if this suits their need, or they may quote from their own *Inspired Version*.

For instance, in support of their doctrine that all men were created as spirits and existed as unembodied spirits in ages past, they will quote Genesis 2:5, 6, which, in their *Inspired Version* reads:

> For I the Lord God created all things of which I

> have spoken, spiritually, before they were naturally upon the face of the earth; for I the Lord God had not caused it to rain upon the face of the earth. And I the Lord God had created all the children of men, and not yet a man to till the ground for in heaven I created them, and there was not yet flesh upon the earth.

Any intelligent reader will know that this is certainly not reliable Scripture. The average person who is not too familiar with the Bible might inadvertently assume that it is. There are scores of distortions of this sort.

The manuscripts of the *Inspired Version* remained in the hands of Joseph's widow, Emma, hence was not published by the Salt Lake Mormons and is not generally used by them. It was first printed in 1866 by the Reorganized Church and is used by them as the basic text of the Bible.

* * *

While this work of "revision" was going on, the Church was expanding rapidly and had now moved to Kirtland, Ohio. Directives were needed for the control of the Church and affairs in general. These took the form of "revelations" and accumulated as a new volume which came to be known as the *Doctrines and Covenants.*[18] They are given as the word

[18] Originally called *Book of Commandments.*

of the Lord received by Joseph Smith. This format was inescapable since Smith had already established the precedent of speaking as God's only appointed prophet.

There is something very incongruous in the subject matter of some of these, such as the paying of printing bills, opening of tanneries and print shops, building a boardinghouse, appointing committees and a host of other mundane matters. A very human source is evident in these "revelations" since only too often the directives backfired to the discredit of Smith and damage to the organization.

* * *

During the Kirtland days, a fourth book was started. This was the *Pearl of Great Price*. This volume is rejected by the Reorganized Church but is a standard text with the Salt Lake Mormons.

The "Book of Moses" which opens the *Pearl of Great Price* is identical to the opening portions of the *Inspired Version* of the Reorganized Church. This volume also contains Matthew 24, quoted with several omissions and changes from the King James Version and appearing under the chapter heading of "Writings of Joseph Smith." This section includes twenty pages of Joseph Smith's own history, and the "Articles of Faith," which appear in several Mormon publications.

The most startling part of the *Pearl of Great Price* is the "Book of Abraham" which Smith describes as:

> A translation of some ancient records, that have fallen into our hands from the catacombs of Egypt; the writings of Abraham while he was in Egypt called the Book of Abraham, written by his own hand upon papyrus.[14]

These papyri were found in the wrappings of certain Egyptian mummies which Smith purchased from a traveling showman named Chandler. The mummy, on which the writings of Abraham were found, was claimed to be that of Pharaoh's daughter.

On pages 50 and 62 of *Pearl of Great Price* are reproductions of pages from the papyrus of the "Book of Abraham." These are given great significance by Smith and their interpretation is outlined in detail. Smith does not claim to have translated these papyri by "revelation" as he had done in his previous writings, but by "translation from the Egyptian."

Smith knew no Egyptian. Even the "reformed Egyptian" of the golden plates had to be "interpreted" by means of the Urim and Thummim. What has been preserved of the "Book of Abraham" bears no resemblance to the "reformed Egyptian" characters of the sample copied by Smith from the golden plates.

[14] *Pearl of Great Price*, p. 50.

Smith no doubt felt quite safe in posing as a translator of the Egyptian since very little was known about the Egyptian language at the time. The first Egyptian grammar, begun by Champollion in the 1820's, was not published until 1836. Developments within the next fifty years (during which Smith's "Book of Abraham" had become gospel to the Mormons) proved that Smith knew nothing of the Egyptian language as is clearly demonstrated in his *Pearl of Great Price.*

The Reorganized Church recognized this and ceased using the book but they did not repudiate its perpetrator.

Egyptologists in the present century have examined Smith's reproductions and declare his "translations" to be utterly incorrect. They agree that Smith's papyri were no more than the ordinary documents used in the funeral rites of the later Egyptian period. There are thousands of these in existence and are on display in any museum of Egyptian antiquities. They insist too that they were not used until at least five hundred years after Abraham's time.

Among these Egyptologists were the eminent scholars: Dr. W. Flinders-Petrie, of London; Dr. James H. Breasted, of Chicago; Dr. Arthur C. Mace, of New York; Dr. John H. Peters, of the University of Pennsylvania; and several others.[15]

[15] Bishop F. S. Spalding, *Joseph Smith, Jr., as a Translator.*

Thus the "Book of Abraham" stands utterly discredited except in the eyes of loyal Mormons. A professor in Brigham Young University, when confronted by these facts by the author, replied, "Mormons would rather trust the inspirations of Joseph Smith than the scholarship of modern scientists."

* * *

A final document, which is considered to be inspired, although not included in the *Doctrines and Covenants,* is a discourse delivered by Joseph Smith before 20,000 of the saints at the funeral of Elder King Follett in Nauvoo, Illinois, in April, 1844.

This Discourse, which was delivered just a few weeks before Smith's murder, gives a final summary of Smith's doctrine of deified man and a humanized god. It is often quoted by Mormons, and from it Lorenzo Snow formulated the cliche: "As man is God was. As God is, man may become."[16]

* * *

The Mormons insist that probably no passage of the Bible has come down to us translated correctly and yet the *Book of Mormon* and Joseph Smith's othe writings contain several thousand verbatim quota tions from the King James Version. These includ at least fifteen full chapters of Isaiah and two chap ters of Malachi. These are in the exact language o

[16] *King Follett Discourse,* p. 9.

the King James Version with all of its sixteenth-century idiom. An examination of Mormon writings reveals that if the quotes and Biblical allusions were excluded, the remainder would be a meaningless jumble of pseudo history.

The Mormons stand accused of two inconsistencies: (1) They have repudiated the very text that is the literary basis of their writings; (2) They have produced out of no creditable source their own scriptures from which they quote endlessly in support of their doctrines. They profess to honor the Bible as a revelation from God for the Eastern Hemisphere while they claim that the *Book of Mormon* is the revelation of God's dealings with the people of the Western Hemisphere.

The Mormons profess a respect for the Bible and sell it in their bookstores, but by their own admission they seldom read it, and dare not expose themselves to its teachings.

Several former Mormons, known to the writer, ascribe their deliverance from the cult to the fact that they had attempted to reconcile Mormonism to the Bible. Their study of the Bible convinced them of the inconsistencies of the Mormon teachings.

CHAPTER TWO

THE MORMONS AND GOD

THE GOD OF THE MORMON THEOLOGY is not the God of the Bible. We may go so far as to say that the god of the present-day Mormon theology is not even the god of the *Book of Mormon.* Mormons squirm when they are told this and become quite evasive when challenged to justify the concept of Deity as it is developed in the writings of their later theologians.

When Joseph Smith was writing the *Book of Mormon,* with the assistance of Oliver Cowdry and Martin Harris (and we suspect, Sidney Rigdon), he and his associates had no greater knowledge of the names and attributes of God than the "average by-stander" of their day.

There was little Biblical exposition available to them in the back country of upper New York State, and the preachers of the area were the camp-meeting exhorters, who themselves knew very little of the plan or structure of the Scriptures.

Calvinism and Arminianism, election and free-will were discussed about as intelligently by the tavernkeepers as they were by the religious-minded. But the teaching of the grace of God in salvation was not being taught by the Calvinists, nor was holy living being practiced, except spasmodically, by the Arminians.

Emotional experiences of any sort were considered as being "conversion" by many. Dreams and visions were commonplace. Many, who scorned the emotionalists, accepted water baptism for the remission of sins as the means of salvation, totally unaware that faith alone is the means of "the remission of sins" and salvation.

There was no knowledge of dispensational teaching, and instructions given by the prophets to Israel in the Old Testament had no distinction from the teachings of Paul to the young churches in Asia Minor and Europe. A quotation from the Bible was equally valid if it was the saying of Satan or Isaiah. The good went to Heaven and the bad went to Hell depending upon their status at the moment of death.

The new church of Alexander Campbell, the adventist groups of William Miller, and the spiritism of the Fox Sisters all grew out of this same soil. Out of this same seed-bed came the *Book of Mormon*, claiming to be a divine revelation but bearing all of the forge marks of an ignorant but highly imaginative and precocious youth, Joseph Smith; his scribe, Oliver Cowdry, doubling as a schoolteacher and a blacksmith; and a local farmer, Martin Harris who was generally successful in business but was a credulous visionary in religious matters.

The person of deity as depicted in the *Book of Mormon* was that of the uninstructed religionist who acknowledged the fact of God as presented by the "exhorters" simply because he did not wish to pose as an atheist. God was taken for granted.

In the *Book of Mormon,* no discernment was exercised in the usage of the several Biblical names of God. The *Eternal God* was used when the *Almighty* was meant. The *Lamb* was used interchangeably with the *Messiah.* The *Most High* was used in connection with Jews, and *Jehovah* with the Gentiles.

As examples of this inconsistency we cite the following. In Mosiah 3:18 (124 B.C.) we find "The Atoning blood of Christ, the Lord Omnipotent." The term "atoning blood of Christ" is out of time sequence in 124 B.C., besides it is non-scriptural and doctrinally incorrect. The only time the word *atonement* is used in connection with the work of Christ is in Romans 5:11, and here it should have been translated "reconciliation." The Greek term "omnipotent" would hardly have been used by the natives of America in 124 B.C.

In Nephi, book one, chapters 11-14 we find the

term "the Lamb of God" used, with 8 variations, 46 times. The term in Scripture is peculiar to the writings of the apostle John and would be completely out of time sequence in 600 B.C. Joseph Smith probably was not conscious of having or not having a definable concept of God while writing the *Book of Mormon*. However, as soon as his new church started to take form, it was necessary for him to develop a theism to fit it.

It must be remembered that by this time Sidney Rigdon, who had in turn been disfellowshipped by the Baptists and Alexander Campbell's new churches, had joined ranks with Smith. There is no evidence that Rigdon was more than a professional theologian. Certainly his knowledge of the text of the Bible was not coupled with any evidence of spiritual discernment. He was merely a religious experimenter who saw in Smith's new religion an opportunity to make a place for himself. Undoubtedly much of Smith's new theology and practically all of the religious phraseology of the several books show Rigdon's influence.

Following the publication of the *Book of Mormon*, Smith's ideas developed rapidly. A thoroughly corporeal God emerged as the *Doctrines and Covenants* started to accumulate and as the *Inspired Version* of the Bible was prepared. By the time the *Pearl of Great Price* was finished, Smith's concept was that of a plurality of gods. By the end of his short lifetime, when he delivered the *King Follett Discourse,* God was one of many gods, and Adam was the god of this world. The gods had become supermen and men had become incipient gods. Smith's theism by this time was a sort of polytheism.

With the raw material of Smith's writings available, it was easy for the followers of the prophet, Brigham Young, Orson and Parley Pratt, Orson Hyde, J. F. Smith, and others to develop the present-day unbiblical Mormon doctrines of deity. The Mormons may be quite sincere in their belief in their god, but he is not the God of the Bible.

A few samples of the development of Smith's theism will be quite enlightening. Three samples from the *Book of Mormon* will suffice to demonstrate that his early concept of God was not particularly unorthodox:

> For I know that God is not a partial God, neither a changeable Being: But he is unchangeable from all eternity to all eternity.[1]
> And Zeezrom said unto him: "Thou sayest there is a true and living God?" And Amulek said: "Yea, there is a true and living God." Now Zeezrom said: "Is there more than one God?" And he answered, "No!"[2]

[1] *Book of Mormon:* Moroni 8:18.
[2] *Book of Mormon:* Alma 11:26-29.

> For do we not read that God is the same yesterday, today and forever, and in him there is no variableness, neither shadow of turning? And now if ye have imagined up unto yourselves a god who doth vary—then have ye imagined up unto yourselves a god who is not a God of miracles—I say unto you he changeth not: If so, he would cease to be God.[3]

We have a suspicion that Mormon was "peeking" when in the fourth century A.D. he was able to quote, verbatim, Hebrews 13:8 and James 1:17 from the seventeenth-century King James Version!

In the early "revelations" recorded in the *Doctrines and Covenants,* which were contemporary with the publication of the *Book of Mormon,* the concept of God had not changed particularly. We read:

> By these things we know that there is a God in heaven who is infinite and eternal, from everlasting the same unchangeable God.[4]
>
> The same unchangeable God, the framer of the heaven and earth . . . gave unto them commandments that they should love and serve him, the only living and true God.[5]

[3] *Book of Mormon:* Mormon 9:8-19.
[4] *Doctrines and Covenants,* 20:17-18.
[5] *Ibid.,* 20:19.

Note by contrast the concept of God as stated in the closing sections of the *Doctrines and Covenants.*[6] We read:

> The Father has a body of flesh and bones as tangible as man's, the Son also.[7]
>
> Then shall they be gods, because they have all power, and the angels are subject unto them.[8]

By the time Joseph Smith prepared the *Pearl of Great Price* he had started the study of Hebrew. He was never a scholar in the Hebrew but gained enough to season his writings and speeches with allusions to it.

He discovered that the term *Elohim,* by which we are introduced to God in Genesis 1, is in the plural form and was used by later writers and non-Biblical writers to express the idea of many gods. This fact he grasped as the final documentation on which to base his "plurality of gods" doctrine. In the "Book of Abraham"[9] he uses the term *the Gods* to translate the Hebrew Elohim in his paraphrase of Genesis 1.

The final step downward in Smith's theism is well expressed in his Discourse at the funeral of Elder King Follett. This was delivered in April, 1844, just

[6] The Utah editions of *Doctrines and Covenants* contain only a few items after the death of Smith. The Reorganized *Doctrines and Covenants* continued to have additions.

[7] *Doctrines and Covenants,* 130:22, Utah editions.

[8] *Ibid.,* 132:20, Utah editions.

[9] *Pearl of Great Price.*

two months before he was murdered by a mob in Carthage, Illinois.

The Reorganized Church has tried to discredit this Discourse in their attempt to evade the Adam-God doctrine which they claim to repudiate. They insist that it was manufactured by the followers of Brigham Young. Their case is rather weak. The Discourse was delivered before an audience of 20,000 and was reported by four scribes: Willard Richards, Wilford Woodruff, Thomas Bullock, and William Clayton. The sermon was delivered in April, 1844. Smith was murdered June 27, 1844, and the King Follett Discourse was published in the August 1, 1844, edition of *Times and Seasons*.

Considering the chaos that resulted after the death of Smith, it is unthinkable that the council of the twelve would have had the time or the inclination to manufacture such a document so unrelated to the stupendous problems that confronted them in those days.

The Mormon theologians have used the King Follett Discourse as Smith's final word on the doctrines of God and man. The following excerpts from the Discourse speak for themselves.[10]

[10] The author's copy of the Discourse is an authentic reprint by Magazine Printing Company, Salt Lake City, Utah and was purchased by the author in Zion's Book Store in Salt Lake City, Utah, in October, 1955.

I am going to inquire after God: for I want you all to know him and be familiar with him. . . . I will go back to the beginning before the world was, to show you what kind of a being God is.

God was once as we are now, and is an exalted man, and sits enthroned in yonder heavens . . . I say, if you were to see him today, you would see him like a man in form—like yourselves in all the person, image, and very form of a man.

I am going to tell you how God came to be God. We have imagined and supposed that God was God from all eternity. I will refute that idea, and take away the veil, so that you may see.

It is the first principle of the gospel to know for certainty the character of God and to know that we may converse with him as one man converses with another, and that he was once a man like us;[11] yea, that God himself, the father of us all, dwelt on an earth, the same as Jesus Christ did.

What did Jesus say? . . . The scripture informs us that Jesus said, "as the Father hath power to himself, even so hath the Son power" . . . to do what? Why, what the Father did. The answer is obvious—in a manner to lay down his body and take it up again.

[11] A footnote to the published edition by Elder B. H. Roberts states: "The doctrine here taught was afterward thrown into the following aphorism by Lorenzo Snow: 'As man now is, God once was. As God is now, man may become.' This form of expressing the truth was doubtless original with Lorenzo Snow, but not the doctrine itself. That is contained in the Prophet's remarks above, text and context."

> Here, then, is eternal life—to know the only wise and true god; and you have got to learn how to be Gods yourselves, and to be kings and priests to God, the same as all Gods have done before you, namely, by going from one small degree to another, and from a small capacity to a great one; from grace to grace, from exaltation to exaltation, until you attain to the resurrection of the dead, and are able to dwell in the everlasting burnings [!], and to sit in glory, as do those who sit enthroned in everlasting power.[12]

Many of the apostles of Joseph Smith, particularly those who followed Brigham Young to Utah, have written and lectured on Smith's concept of God, and while these are not considered "inspired" by the Church, they are considered authoritative. Much has been written to confirm Smith's doctrines by the several presidents of the Church. The presidency of the Mormon Church carries with it the power to receive "revelations" with as much authority as the Romanists claim for the Pope when he speaks ex cathedra, so we may take these utterances as being the authoritative teachings of the Mormons. Here are some samples:

> Question: Are there more Gods than one?
> Answer: Yes, many.[13]

[12] *King Follett Discourse,* pp. 8, 9, 10.
[13] Elder John Jacques, *Catechism,* 14:13.

> In the beginning, the head of the gods called a council of the gods; and they came together and concocted a plan to create the world and people it.[14]

> Remember that God our heavenly Father was perhaps once a child, and mortal like we are, and rose step by step in the scale of progress, in the school of advancement; has moved forward and overcome until he has arrived at the point where he now is.[15]

> Mormon prophets have continuously taught the sublime truth that God the Eternal Father was once a mortal man who passed through a school of earth similar to that through which we are passing. He became God—an exalted being.[16]

> Mormonism does not tend to debase God to the level of man, but to exalt man to the perfection of God.[17]

This last utterance would certainly please Satan who first coined the idea in the Garden of Eden. Satan said unto the woman, "Ye shall be as gods."[18]

Probably the most blasphemous of all, and one

[14] Joseph Smith, *Journal of Discourse,* Vol. VI, p. 5.

[15] Orson Hyde, *Journal of Discourse,* Vol. I, p. 123.

[16] Milton R. Hunter, *Gospel Through the Ages,* p. 104.

[17] Charles W. Penrose, *Millennial Star,* Vol. 23, p. 181.

[18] Genesis 3:5.

that some later apologists have tried to tone down, is the early expression of Brigham Young:

> Now hear it, O inhabitants of the earth, Jew and Gentile, saint and sinner. When our father, Adam, came into the Garden of Eden, he came into it with a celestial body, and brought Eve, one of his wives, with him. He helped to make and organize this world. He is Michael, the archangel, the Ancient of Days about whom holy men have written and spoken. He is our Father and our God, and the only God with whom we have to do.[19]

On this occasion Young, no doubt, felt himself to be on safe ground since this statement is no more than a commentary on Smith's own words as expressed in Section 27 of the *Doctrines and Covenants*: "And also Michael, or Adam, the Father of all, the prince of all, the Ancient of Days."

It is quite obvious that Joseph Smith's concept of God, and that of his disciples, has followed the pattern of the deterioration of the gentile concept of God as outlined by Paul in Romans 1:21-26. This deterioration in doctrine parallels a corresponding pattern of deterioration in morals. It is observable that no system of religion postulates a god having a stature higher than the moral practices of its adherents. We do not say that Mormonism has gone all

[19] Brigham Young, *Journal of Discourses*, Vol. I, p. 50.

the way to the bottom in Paul's scale, but we do say that several steps downward are discernible.

1. Note what Paul says. "They knew God," which is the original position of mankind in his proper appreciation of the nature of God. "They worshiped him not as God."

2. "Their foolish heart was darkened."

3. "Professing themselves to be wise, they became fools." Man considers his thoughts to be equal to the thoughts of God.

4. "They changed the glory of the uncorruptible God into the likeness of corruptible man"; this is the emergence of the corporeal god.

5. "God gave them up to vile passions."

We are not saying that the polygamous practices of the Mormons are on the low scale of the sex perversions described by Paul and practiced by the idolaters of paganism. We do say that their polygamy is taught as having a religious significance. Sex worship, such as was present in Baalism, is only one step lower on the scale of deterioration.

In the history of man's religions it is always observable that three developments occur almost coincidentally: (1) The emergence of a corporeal god; (2) The deification of man; and (3) The development of sexual irregularities, usually as acts of worship. This is what Paul is saying in the Roman letter. This is the status of the Mormon theism.

The Mormons have a perfect right to worship such a god if they wish; but we repeat: This is not the God of the Bible.

CHAPTER THREE

THE MORMONS AND THE TRINITY

THE OPENING ITEM of the Mormon statement of faith says:

> We believe in God the eternal Father and in his son Jesus Christ and in the Holy Ghost.

This, superficially, would seem to be a satisfactory trinitarian statement. But must we take it for granted that this is the Mormon meaning of the statement?

The Mormons do not believe in a triune Godhead. Their statement of faith, if it reflects anything of their belief, provides primarily for three separate gods, completely apart from the orthodox Christian belief in a triune God. Commentaries indicating that we are not misstating their case are abundant. These many statements also indicate clearly that the Mormon teaching of a corporeal god is standard in their thinking.

The first vision claimed by Joseph Smith reveals this fact. Here are the circumstances leading up to the reception of the vision. Smith says:

> There was in the place where we lived an unusual excitement on the subject of religion. . . . The whole district . . . seemed affected by it, and great multitudes united themselves to the different religious parties, which created no small stir and division amongst the people, some crying, "Lo here!" and others, "Lo there!" Some were contending for the Methodist faith, some for the Presbyterian, and some for the Baptist. . . . I was at this time in my fifteenth year. My father's family was proselyted to the Presbyterian faith.
>
> During this time . . . my mind was called up to serious reflection and great uneasiness; but though my feelings were deep and often poignant, still I kept myself aloof from all these parties though I attended their several meetings. . . . My mind became somewhat partial to the Methodist sect, and I felt some desire to be united with them; but so great was the confusion and strife among the different denominations, that it was impossible for a person young as I was . . . to come to any certain conclusion who was right and who was wrong.
>
> While I was laboring under the extreme difficulties caused by the contests of these parties of

religionists, I was one day reading the Epistle of James, first chapter and fifth verse which reads: "If any of you lack wisdom, let him ask of God, that giveth to all men liberally, and upbraideth not: and it shall be given him!"

Never did any passage of scripture come with more power . . . it seemed to enter with great force into every feeling of my heart. . . . At length I came to the conclusion that I must either remain in darkness and confusion, or else I must do as James directs . . . so in accordance with this . . . I retired to the woods to make the attempt. . . . After I had retired to the place where I had previously designed to go, having looked around me, and finding myself alone, I kneeled down and began to offer up the desires of my heart to God.

I was seized upon by some power which entirely overcame me, and had such an astonishing influence over me as to bind my tongue so that I could not speak. Much darkness gathered around me, and it seemed to me for a time as if I were doomed to sudden destruction.

But, exerting all my powers to call upon God to deliver me out of the power of this enemy which had seized upon me, and at the very moment when I was ready to sink into despair and abandon myself to destruction—not to an imaginary ruin, but to the power as I had never before felt in any being —just at this moment of great alarm, I saw a pillar of light exactly over my head, above the brightness

> of the sun, which descended gradually until it fell upon me.
>
> It no sooner appeared than I found myself delivered from the enemy which held me bound. When the light rested upon me I saw two personages, whose brightness and glory defy all description, standing above me in the air. One of them spake unto me, calling me by name and said, pointing to the other—"This is my beloved son, hear him." [1]

This vision was not mentioned by Smith until several years after it was supposed to have occurred. There are those who argue that Joseph never had such a vision but that he conjured it up in order to substantiate his later theology. We recognize the logic of those who reason this way since there is much evidence in his writings of "ex post facto" revelation. My own opinion is that if this first vision has been reported accurately, it corresponds to the method by which Satan can transform himself into an angel of light.

Someone may raise the question, "Would one praying for light, as Smith claims to have done, be answered by a satanic seizure and vision?" Our answer would be that Joseph Smith had the Word of God before him, but failed to correlate the Bible with the vision that he claimed to have had. Thus, since he sought for light apart from the

[1] *Pearl of Great Price*, pp. 84, 85.

Word of God, he was answered by a revelation that does not tally with the Word of God. The Spirit of God speaks through the Word of God (John 17:17).

If Joseph Smith had continued his reading to James 1:18 he would have had an authentic revelation of God's process of salvation. This verse says, "Of his own will begat he us with the word of truth."

John Henry Evans, an apologist of Smith's, insists that it was hopeless for a boy of fourteen to expect to get any help from the study of the Bible.[2] This is obviously an inconsistent conclusion since the Mormons themselves consider a person to be at an age of accountability sufficient for baptism at the age of eight, and capable of undertaking the office of deacon at fourteen.

The revelation that serves as a commentary on the nature of this first vision of Smith's reads as follows:

> The Father has a body of flesh and bones as tangible as man's; the Son also: but the Holy Ghost has not a body of flesh and bones, but is a personage of spirit. Were it not so, the Holy Ghost could not dwell in us.[3]

J. E. Talmage, one of the foremost of the later Mormon expositors, gives several comments on the

[2] John Henry Evans, *An American Prophet*, p. 345.
[3] *Doctrines and Covenants*, 130:22.

Mormon view of the Trinity, as distinguished from the Christian view. He says:

> Three persons composing the great presiding council have revealed themselves to man: 1) God the eternal Father, 2) His son Jesus Christ, 3) the Holy Ghost—these three are separate individuals, physically distinct from each other.[4]

There is probably no greater document expressing the doctrine of the Trinity than that formulated in the Nicene creed. Of this J. E. Talmage says: "It would be difficult to conceive of a greater number of inconsistencies and contradictions expressed in words so few."[5]

This same author commenting on the much simpler statement in the confessional of the Church of England remarks: "The immateriability of God as is asserted in these declarations of sectarian faith is entirely at variance with the scriptures, and absolutely contradicted by the revelations of God's person and attributes. The Church of Jesus Christ of Latter-day Saints proclaims against the incomprehensible God devoid of body, parts or passions as a thing impossible of existence, and asserts its belief in and allegiance to the true and living God of scripture and revelations."[6]

[4] James E. Talmage, *The Articles of Faith,* p. 39.
[5] *Ibid.,* p. 48.
[6] *Ibid.,* p. 48.

One of the most noted of the Mormon theologians was Parley P. Pratt. Pratt's greatest work is his *Key to the Science of Theology*. Mormons do not question his writings. One of Pratt's comments on the doctrine of the Trinity is as follows:

> Among these theories [the doctrines of the Christian church] we will notice one which is, perhaps, more extensively received by different sects than any other. The language runs thus, "There is one only living and true God, without body, parts or passions; consisting of three persons, the Father, Son and Holy Ghost."
>
> It is painful to the human mind to be compelled to admit that such wonderful inconsistencies of language or ideas have ever found place in human creed. . . . It is but another way of saying that there is a God who does not exist, a God who is composed of nonentity, who is the negative of all existence, who occupies no space, who exists in no time, who is composed of no substance. . . . Such a God could never be seen, heard or felt by any being in the universe.[7]

Obviously Pratt and the Mormons have excluded the possibility of thinking beyond the realm of the physical or the visible. Pratt demonstrates this as he continues:

> There never has been a visible idol worshipped

[7] Parley P. Pratt, *Key to the Science of Theology*, pp. 28, 29.

> among men which was so powerless as this "God without body, passions or parts.
> "The God of Egypt, the crocodile, could destroy.
> "The Peruvian God, the sun, could diffuse its genial warmth, light and influence."[8]

Thus Pratt accords the sun god and the crocodile of Egypt a higher place than the eternal Trinity of the Bible.

Pratt also comments on the nature of the Father and the Son. He says:

> "Jesus Christ and His Father are two persons, in the same sense as John and Peter are two persons. Each of them has an organized, individual tabernacle embodied in material form, and composed of material substances in the likeness of man and possessing every organ, limit and physical part that man possesses."[9]

Pratt does not comment at this point on the relationship of the Holy Spirit to the Trinity. His theories regarding this subject will be discussed in a later chapter.

[8] *Ibid.*
[9] *Ibid.*, p. 34.

CHAPTER FOUR

THE MORMONS AND JESUS CHRIST

"WHAT THINK YE OF CHRIST?" is still the supreme test of orthodox Christianity. The Lord accepted Peter's confession: "Thou art the Christ, the Son of the living God" and on the basis of this confession is built the structure of the Church.[1]

The Holy Spirit inspired the beloved disciple to pen the lines which declare, in no uncertain terms, the facts of the eternal deity of our Lord. John's Gospel introduces Him as the Word of God who was coequal and coeternal with the Father, and as the One by whom everything was created.[2] This same Gospel introduces the fact of the Incarnation as the step by which Deity assumed a veil of human flesh

[1] Matthew 16:13-18.
[2] John 1:1-3.

in order that He might reveal the Godhead in terms that man could understand. Having done this, He offered Himself as the only Substitute for lost man that would be acceptable for man's redemption in God's sight.[3] Jesus Himself claimed deity.

Speaking to the Jews in the Temple He claimed to be the eternal One who was before Abraham. He said, "Before Abraham was I Am" (Greek: *ego eimi*).[4] In using this form of the verb *to be* He identifies Himself with the One who revealed Himself to Moses as the self-existent One. This One instructed Moses when He appeared to him in the burning bush to tell Israel that "I Am hath sent me unto you."[5]

Thus the One who spoke to the Jews at the Feast of Tabernacles was the same One who spoke to Moses and identified Himself as the eternal One, that is, Jehovah.

In the upper-room discourse He identified Himself as being One with the Father. He said: "He that hath seen me hath seen the Father."[6] In His great high priestly prayer He claimed pre-existence and coequality with the Father when He said: "Glorify

[3] John 1:9-14.
[4] John 8:56-58.
[5] Exodus: 3:14.
[6] John 14:7-11.

thou me . . . with the glory which I had with thee before the world was."[7]

John, in stating the reason for writing his Gospel, said: "These [things] are written, that ye might believe that Jesus is the Christ, the Son of God; and that believing ye might have life through his name."[8]

Concerning His manhood, the Word declares that He was begotten by the Holy Ghost of a virgin mother.[9] The Word teaches His impeccability. We read that He "did no sin,"[10] He "knew no sin,"[11] and "in him was no sin."[12]

The Word teaches us that His death was voluntary. Jesus said: "I lay down my life, that I might take it again. No man taketh it from me, but I lay it down of myself. I have power to lay it down, and I have power to take it again."[13]

The Word teaches that Jesus was raised from the dead without seeing corruption.[14] It teaches that He was raised from the dead physically. It teaches that His resurrection is the evidence of the validity of His work of redemption, and that only through His

[7] John 17:5.
[8] John 20:31.
[9] Matthew 1:20, 21; Luke 1:35.
[10] I Peter 2:22.
[11] II Corinthians 5:21.
[12] I John 3:5.
[13] John 10:17, 18.
[14] Acts 2:27; 13:35-37.

resurrection is salvation from the penalty of sin assured to us.[15]

We do not hesitate to state that in each of these propositions Jesus Christ is unique. We state further that each of these truths is vital and central to the teachings of orthodox Christianity.

The Mormons, in one way or another, deny all of these propositions. They deny that the "Word," who became flesh, was unique in His eternality and coequality with God by making Him merely one of the spirits of men, gods, and demons who existed coequally and coeternally with God.

The following statements, culled from many, will suffice to state the Mormon position.

> Man is a spirit clothed with a tabernacle the intelligent part of which was never created or made but existed eternally—man was also in the beginning with God.[16]
>
> He [man] existed before he came to earth: He was with God "in the beginning." Man's destiny is divine. Man is an eternal being. He also is "from everlasting to everlasting."[17]
>
> Jesus Christ is not the father of the spirits who have taken or will take bodies, for He is one of them. He is the son and they are the sons and daughters of Elohim.[18]

[15] I Corinthians 15:1-14; Romans 4:25.
[16] J. F. Smith, *Progress of Man*, pp. 9-11.
[17] John A. Widtsoe, *Varieties of American Religion*, p. 132.
[18] James E. Talmage, p. 473.

We have a succession of gods from Adam down to Christ (his son) and his apostles at least all men, including Jesus Christ, being in the image of his father, and possessing a similar knowledge of good and evil.[19]

If I can pass Brother Joseph, I shall stand a good chance for passing Peter, Jesus and the prophets.[20]

As for the Devil and his fellow spirits, they are brothers to man and also to Jesus and sons and daughters of God in the same sense that we are.[21]

There is no impropriety . . . in speaking of Jesus Christ as the elder brother of the rest of human kind.[22]

The Mormons teach that Jesus was the natural born child of Adam and Mary:

When the Virgin Mary conceived the child Jesus . . . he was not begotten by the Holy Ghost. And who is his Father? He is the first of the human family.[23]

Jesus, our elder brother, was begotten in the flesh by the same character that was in the garden of Eden.[24]

19 Richards, *Millennial Star*, 17:195-6.
20 Young, *Journal of Discourses*, Vol. IV, p. 271.
21 John Henry Evans, *An American Prophet*, p. 241.
22 James E. Talmage, *Articles of Faith*, p. 473.
23 Young, *Journal of Discourses*, pp. 50-51.
24 *Ibid.*

The Mormons believe that Jesus was not unique in His birth, boyhood, or manhood.

> Jesus Christ, a little babe like all the rest of us, grew to be a man, was filled with a divine substance or fluid, called the Holy Spirit, by which he comprehended and spake the truth.[25]

The Mormons see no more in the life of Jesus than in any of us. Elder B. H. Roberts in a footnote to Joseph Smith's *King Follett Discourse,* quoting Sir Oliver Lodge as an authority on the subject states:

> His humanity is to be recognized as real and ordinary—whatever happened to him may happen to any one of us.
>
> The divinity of Jesus, and the divinity of all other noble and stately souls, in so far as they, too, have been influenced by a spark of Deity—can be recognized as manifestations of the Divine.[26]

The Mormons see no uniqueness in the resurrection of Jesus Christ except in the fact that His resurrection preceded others. It has nothing to do with our salvation or justification. Pratt in his *Key to the Science of Theology* says:

> Every man who is eventually made perfect, raised from the dead, and filled or quickened with a fullness of celestial glory, will become like them

[25] Parley P. Pratt, *Key to the Science of Theology,* p. 30.
[26] *King Follett Discourse,* p. 11.

> (the Father and the son) in every respect, physically and in intellect, attributes and powers.[27]

The Mormons teach that man is not saved by the redemptive work of Christ or through the shedding of His blood on Calvary. They believe rather that:

> The very germs of these Godlike attributes (of the Father and son) being engendered in man, the offspring of Deity, only need cultivating, improving, developing and advancing by means of a series of changes, in order to arrive at the fountain head, the standard, the climax of Divine Humanity.[28]

* * *

The Mormons believe that Jesus Christ was a polygamist. This is inescapable. The whole system of Mormon progress in life to come is based on the sealing of marriages in this life. Unmarried people, and couples whose marriages are not sealed by the temple endowments become angels. Those sealed for eternity become gods.[29]

Jesus Christ according to Mormon doctrine[30] was no more divine before His Incarnation than any of us. Thus according to Mormon logic if Jesus was not married during His earthly life, He could rise no higher than an angel in the next life.

27 Pratt, *Key to the Science of Theology,* p. 32.
28 *Ibid.,* p. 32.
29 *Doctrines and Covenants,* 132.
30 John Henry Evans, *An American Prophet,* p. 241.

The Mormons insist that Jesus was married at Cana of Galilee. Orson Hyde says:

> If at the marriage of Cana of Galilee, Jesus was the bridegroom and took unto him Mary, Martha and the other Mary, it shocks not our nerves. If there was not attachment and familiarity between our Saviour and these women, highly proper only in the relation of husband and wife, then we have no sense of propriety.[31]

Later on speaking on this same theme, Hyde says:

> If he never married, his intimacy with Mary and Martha, and the other Mary also, whom Jesus loved, must have been highly unbecoming and improper to say the best of it.[32]

The Mormons teach that Jesus had children before His crucifixion. This of course follows in the Mormon line of reasoning, otherwise Jesus could not have complete exaltation in the next life. On this point Hyde teaches:

> Did he multiply, and did he see his seed? Did he know his Father's law by complying with it, or did he not? Others may do as they like, but I will not charge our Saviour with neglect or transgression in this or any other duty.[33]

31 Orson Hyde, *Journal of Discourses*, Vol. II, pp. 81-82.
32 *Ibid.*, Vol. IV, p. 259.
33 *Ibid.*, p. 259.

Hyde continues in another sermon:

> We say it was Jesus Christ who was married whereby He could see His seed before He was crucified. I shall say here that before the Saviour died He looked upon His own natural children as we look upon ours. When Mary came to the sepulchre she saw two angels and she said unto them "they have taken away my Lord or husband."[34]

The Mormons use the name of Jesus Christ in the title of their Church, but any discerning Christian will readily observe that this is not the Jesus Christ whom we worship as the eternal Son of God who died for our sins according to the Scriptures. Theirs is not the Christ of whom Peter said:

> Neither is there salvation in any other: for there is none other name under heaven given among men, whereby we must be saved.[35]

Neither is theirs the Saviour of whom Paul said: "Who was delivered for our offenses, and was raised again for our justification. Therefore being justified by faith, we have peace with God through our Lord Jesus Christ."[36]

[34] *Ibid.*, p. 210.
[35] Acts 4:12.
[36] Romans 4:25–5:1.

CHAPTER FIVE

THE MORMONS AND THE HOLY SPIRIT

THERE IS NO PHASE of Christian doctrine that requires more careful and discerning study than the subject of the Person and work of the Holy Spirit.

For the purpose of establishing a standard of measurement by which to evaluate the Mormon concept of this doctrine, we make the following statement. This will satisfy, we believe, all truly orthodox Christians.[1]

1. The Holy Spirit is identified in Scripture as having a distinct personality and is not merely an "influence."

[1] William Evans, *The Great Doctrines of the Bible,* pp. 107 ff.

a. He is referred to in the third person, masculine gender, singular: He, Him, His (John 14:17; 15:26; 16:24).
b. Ananias lied to the Holy Spirit. One cannot lie to an influence (Acts 5:3, 4).
c. The Holy Spirit gave instruction for the ordination of Paul and Barnabas. An influence could not do this (Acts 13:2).

2. The Holy Spirit is identified in His relationship to the Trinity as being coequal and coeternal with the Father and the Son (Gen. 1:1; 1:26; 11:7; Isa. 6:8; 48:13-16; Matt. 3:16; 28:19; John 15:26; II Cor. 13:14; Eph. 2:18; I John 5:7; Heb. 9:14).

3. The Holy Spirit is identified as having the attributes of Deity.

a. Eternality—Hebrews 9:14.
b. Omnipotence—Psalm 104:30.
c. Omnipresence—Psalm 139:7.
d. Omniscience—Isaiah 40:13; I Corinthians 2:10, 11.

4. As to the work or ministry of the Holy Spirit, the Bible indicates the following:

a. The Holy Spirit is the author of the Word of God (II Peter 1:21; II Tim. 3:16).
b. He is the "architect" of the universe (Gen. 1:2, 3, 26; Job 26:13; Ps. 104:30).

c. He is the agent of the Trinity in the dealings of God with man.
   (1) In Genesis 6:3 He strives with man.
   (2) In Job 32:8 He gives enlightenment.
   (3 In Exodus 31:2-5 He imparts skill.
   (4) In Judges 14:6 He gives physical vigor.
   (5) In Numbers 11:25; Judges 11:29; II Peter 1:21; II Samuel 23:2 He empowers the servants of God.

d. The Holy Spirit is the agent of the new birth.
   (1) In John 16:7-14 He convicts and enlightens concerning sin, righteousness and judgment.
   (2) In John 3:5, 6 He regenerates.
   (3) In Ephesians 1:13, 14 He seals the believers.
   (4) In I Corinthians 12:3 He baptizes the believers into one Body, the Church.

e. The Holy Spirit activates and empowers believers as individuals, or collectively as the Church.
   (1) In John 14:17; Romans 8:9-11 He indwells.
   (2) In John 14:26; 16:13; Romans 8:14; I John 2:20-27 He instructs.
   (3) In Romans 8:26, 27 He intercedes between man and the Father in matters of intercession and supplication.
   (4 In Romans 8:4 He empowers the believer to walk the walk of faith.
   (5) The Holy Spirit is the custodian of the

Church while on this earth and until the home-call of the Body of Christ (John 14:16; II Thess. 2:16, 17; Rev. 22:17).

One could go on endlessly outlining the various aspects of the Person and work of the Holy Spirit but the above outline should suffice for purposes of comparison between the Christian and the Mormon concepts.

Now let us examine the Mormon attitude.

The first item of the Mormon doctrinal statement simply states: "We believe in God the Eternal Father, and in His Son Jesus Christ and in the Holy Ghost." This could mean anything. In *Doctrines and Covenants* we read the following:

> The Father has a body of flesh and bones as tangible as man's the Son also: but the Holy Ghost has not a body of flesh and bones but is a personage of spirit.[2]

That some of the Mormon expositors had variable convictions concerning the identity of the Holy Spirit, as a Person, is shown by their writers. Orson Pratt remarks:

> I am inclined to think, from some things in the revelations, that there is such a personal being as a personal Holy Ghost, but it is not set forth as a positive fact, and the Lord has never given me any

[2] *Doctrines and Covenants,* 130:22.

revelation upon the subject and consequently I cannot make up my mind one way or the other.[3]

Orson Pratt's concept came to conform to that of his contemporaries in his later expressions. One of his later statements reads:

> No two persons can receive the same identical particles of this spirit at the same time; a part thereof of the Holy Spirit will rest upon one man and another part upon another.[4]

Mormons always refer to the Holy Spirit as *it* and in the most casual manner. I have heard a Mormon Melchizedek priest remark that Satan makes use of the Holy Spirit using "its" power in a bad way.

Parley Pratt, brother of Orson, expresses the subject in a fashion that reflects the thinking of the Mormon teachers. This will be accepted by all Mormons as orthodox teaching. Parley Pratt says:

> This substance, like all others, is one of the elements of material, or physical existence, and therefore subject to the necessary laws which govern all matter. Like all other matters, its whole is composed of individual particles. Like them, each particle occupies space, possesses the power of motion, requires time to move from one place to another, and can in no wise occupy two spaces at once. In

[3] Orson Pratt, *Journal of Discourses*, Vol. II.

[4] Orson Pratt, *Absurdities of Materialism*, a pamphlet, p. 24.

these respects it differs nothing from all other matter. It penetrates the pores of the most solid substances, pierces the human system to its most inward recesses, discerns the thoughts and intents of the heart. It has power to move through space with inconceivable velocity, far exceeding the tardy motions of electricity or of physical light. It comprehends the past present and future in all their fullness. It is endowed with knowledge, wisdom, truth, love, charity, justice, and mercy in all their ramifications.[5]

Mormons deny that the Lord Jesus was conceived in the womb of the Virgin Mary by the Holy Spirit. Joseph Smith laid the ground work for the doctrine by establishing Adam as a deity.[6]

Brigham Young follows logically by declaring:

"When the Virgin Mary conceived the child Jesus, the Father had begotten him in his own likeness. He was not begotten by the Holy Ghost, and who is his father? He is the first of the human family—now remember from this time forth, and forever, that Jesus Christ was not begotten by the Holy Ghost."[7]

What a contrast between the blasphemous views

[5] Parley P. Pratt, *Key to the Science of Theology*, pp. 39-40.
[6] *Doctrines and Covenants* 27:11, 78:16, 107:54, 116:1.
[7] Brigham Young, *Journal of Discourses*, Vol. 1, pp. 50-51.

of the Mormons and the crystal-clear statements of Scripture! Matthew's Gospel says:

> The angel of the Lord appeared unto him in a dream, saying . . . fear not to take unto thee Mary thy wife: for that which is conceived in her is of the Holy Ghost.[8]

Luke's Gospel records:

> And the angel answered and said unto her, The Holy Ghost shall come upon thee, and the power of the Highest shall overshadow thee: therefore also that holy thing that shall be born of thee shall be called the Son of God.[9]

The failure of Mormons to understand the true nature of the Holy Spirit as a Person, and yet totally nonphysical, is a result of their concept of the Godhead as being composed of separate physical Persons. They reason thus: If God the Father and Jesus Christ His Son are separate "personages of flesh and bones," how can a Person of the Godhead be pure spirit and still be a Person? Thus the Spirit, in their thinking, must be an element dispensed in varying qualities to each individual.

They cannot accept the Christian doctrine of the indwelling Spirit of God, who indwells believers subsequent to the new birth, thereby indwelling

[8] Matthew 1:20.
[9] Luke 1:35.

the Body of Christ, the Church. They cannot conceive of the Holy Spirit as being universally resident in believers. They say: "How can a personal Holy Spirit be indwelling separate people at the same time?"[10] This same sort of reasoning is responsible for their concept of God the Father as being not purely "spirit." Joseph Fielding Smith in commenting on the statement made by the Lord Jesus to the woman of Sychar that "God is a spirit"[11] says: "This I do not believe."[12]

James L. Barker in *The Divine Church* with this same limited concept says: " 'No man hath seen God at any time' [John 1:18] is not in harmony with other scriptures." He reasons that "in such cases, either the text has not come down correctly to the present or it has been incorrectly translated."[13]

The failure of Mormon thought with relation to the oneness of the Trinity and at the same time the personality of the Spirit is due to their failure to understand that all of the divine propositions cannot be confined within the limits of human expression.

Joseph Smith implies in the *Pearl of Great Price* that since God spoke "face to face" with Moses, that Moses was looking at a physical personage with

[10] Orson Pratt, *Absurdities of Materialism.*
[11] John 4:24.
[12] Joseph Fielding Smith, *Teachings of Joseph Smith,* p. 85.
[13] James L. Barker, *The Divine Church,* p. 9.

physical eyes. The phrase "face to face" is the Hebrew expression conveying intimacy between Moses and God. The Bible is full of such *anthropomorphisms*. This does not imply that God is corporeal but indicates that He communicated Himself in expressions with which men were familiar. Thus Joseph Smith had to reject the later statement in Exodus 33:20, "Thou canst not see my face . . . and live" as a contradiction to the previous statement that "the Lord spake unto Moses face to face." The only difficulty here is in the paucity of human language or rather in Smith's inability to understand the significance of the scriptural language and values.

Joseph Smith and most Mormons insist on confining their interpretation of given portions of Scripture within the limitations of the semantics of the King James English.

CHAPTER SIX

THE MORMON DOCTRINE OF MAN

SATAN WAS A CONSERVATIVE compared with Joseph Smith when he said to Eve, "Ye shall be as gods."[1] Joseph Smith and his theologians leave out the *as*. They promise deity to all of the faithful. Smith stated it thus:

> You have got to learn how to be Gods yourselves —the same as all the Gods have done before you.[2]

In order to elevate man to the status of a god it was necessary for Smith to lower the stature of his god. He does this by stating: "God . . . was once a man like us."[3] Given this latitude, the Mormon theologians enlarged on the idea and developed their present concept of man as a potential god.

[1] Genesis 3:5.
[2] *King Follett Discourse,* p. 10.
[3] *Ibid.,* p. 9.

Lorenzo Snow, a contemporary of Joseph Smith, codified Smith's teaching in the following aphorism, which is now standard with Mormon teachers:

> As man is, God was.
> As God is, man may become.[4]

Another contemporary of Smith's, recognized by the Mormons as one of their greatest theologians, said:

> Remember that God our heavenly Father was perhaps once a child, and mortal like we are, and rose step by step in the scale of progress, in the school of advancement; has moved forward and overcome until he has arrived at the point where he now is.[5]

Having thus reduced the stature of Deity to that of an elevated superman, the Mormon teachers have had little trouble developing a "doctrine of man" that places man on a par with such a Deity. Needless to say, the Mormon god is not the God of the Bible nor is the Mormon "man" the creature who came from the hand of an almighty and eternal God.

In order to develop such a God-man theory it was necessary for the Mormons to develop their own

[4] *Millennial Star,* Vol. 54. Milton R. Hunter, *Gospel Through the Ages,* pp. 105-106.

[5] Orson Hyde, *Journal of Discourses,* Vol. I, p. 123.

particular doctrine of reincarnation. Not that this is new with them, they have merely changed some of the wording.

First they teach that all human beings and spirits, and even Jesus Christ and Satan, existed as spirit beings from an eternity past. At physical birth, the spirits are given bodies in which they can exercise their choices of right and wrong. Thus the present life is a period of probation. The manner in which this probationary period is utilized, determines completely the status of the individual in the next life after the resurrection.

The afterlife starts in where the present life leaves off. If the deeds and accomplishments in this life have been satisfactory and all temple endowments have been fulfilled, the individual becomes a god and is considered eligible to go on to create and populate worlds of his own, and so on ad infinitum. No good Mormon will deny that this is standard Mormon doctrine. But lest someone question the accuracy of our statements, we will quote from standard and approved Mormon theologians.

Joseph Smith prepared the way for the later Mormon teachers when he rewrote the Creation story. This material he placed in his "Book of Moses" which reads the same in the *Pearl of Great Price,* which the Salt Lake Mormons use, and in the *In-*

spired Version as used by the Reorganized Church. Smith says:

> For I, the Lord God, created all things of which I have spoken, spiritually, before they were naturally upon the face of the earth—for in heaven I created them—and man became a living soul, the first flesh upon the earth—the first man also; nevertheless, all things were before created: but spiritually were they created and made according to my word.[6]

In this same volume Smith has the Lord saying to Enoch:

> Anoint thine eyes with clay and wash them and thou shalt see. And he did so. And he beheld the spirits that God had created, and he beheld also things which were not visible to the natural eye.[7]

A few months later, certainly not later than 1835 Joseph Smith had prepared the final "chapters" of his "scriptures." These he called the "Book of Abraham," and claims to have translated them from papyri found on a mummy purchased from a traveling showman, Michael N. Chandler.[8]

There were four mummies in the collection. One

[6] "Book of Moses" 3:5-7, *Pearl of Great Price,* p. 12; *Inspired Version,* "Moses" 3:5-7.

[7] *Ibid.*. "Moses" 6:34-35.

[8] *Handbook of Reference,* p. 45.

of these was ascertained to be that of Pharaoh's daughter (Fourteenth Dynasty) another was that of Pharaoh Necho (Twenty-sixth Dynasty). On the mummy of Pharaoh's daughter were papyri which consisted of the handwriting of Abraham (Eleventh Dynasty). From this Eleventh Dynasty papyrus found on a Fourteenth Dynasty mummy, purchased together with a Twenty-eighth Dynasty mummy, Joseph Smith translated his "Book of Abraham."

Be it said to the credit of the Reorganized Church, that when the hoax was exposed by competent Egyptologists, they repudiated the "Book of Abraham." The balance of the *Pearl of Great Price* they must accept since it is the identical matter found in the *Inspired Version*. One wonders how they can reject Smith's hoax without rejecting Smith.

In this "Book of Abraham" we read (and here I quote quite at length):

> Now the Lord had shown unto me, Abraham, the intelligences that were organized before the world was: and among all these there were many of the noble and great ones;
>
> And God saw these souls that were good, and he stood in the midst of them, and he said: These I will make my rulers; for he stood among those that were spirits and he saw that they were good; and he said unto me: Abraham, thou art one of them; thou wast chosen before thou wast born.

> And there stood one among them that was like unto God[9] and he said unto those who were with him: we will go down, for there is space there, and we will take of these materials and we will make an earth where on these may dwell.
>
> And the Lord said: whom shall I send? And one answered like unto the Son of Man: Here am I, send me. And another answered, and said: Here am I send me. And the Lord said: I will send the first.
>
> And the second was angry and kept not his first estate, and at that day, many followed after him.[10]

With this pseudo-Biblical background the Mormon theologians have gone to work in real earnest to develop the theory.

Students of church history will recognize, as we go along, a similarity to the "precreated spirits" doctrine of Origen and others. I doubt if Smith ever heard of Origen and his heresies, although Rigdon may have been acquainted with Origen's theory. Later teachers among Mormons do use Origen's writings to confirm their teaching, but I believe Smith reached his conclusions in the same manner

9 Here a footnote refers back to a passage in the "Book of Moses" that obviously refers to the Son of God, thus making Him a precreated Spirit.

10 This obviously refers to Satan whom the Mormons make to be a disobedient spirit and a brother spirit with Jesus Christ. This is one of their proof texts.

as Origen, by theorizing in an area in which the Bible is silent. Commenting on such theorizers Lewis Sperry Chafer says:

> There is much room where God has not spoken for theologians to fill in large portions wholly agreeable to their way of thinking; then in later developments of their system, they draw out of their own creation precisely what they have prepared and need.[11]

This precisely, is the practice of Smith and all of the Mormon commentators.

Following are a few of the developments of the doctrine by later Mormon writers:

> Jesus Christ is not the father of the spirits who have taken or yet shall take bodies upon this earth, for he is one of them.[12]
>
> It is the belief of the Latter-day Saints that the earth was organized in order that personages of spirit—the spiritual children of God—might have a place where they could take upon themselves mortality—take mortal bodies. It was necessary for them to become mortal before they could learn good from evil, joy from sorrow. It was necessary to become mortal in order to have increase, children to learn the ways of God and obey his laws.[13]

11 Lewis Sperry Chafer, *Systematic Theology*, Vol. II, p. 169.
12 James E. Talmage, *Articles of Faith*, p. 473.
13 Bardella Shipp Curtis, *Sacred Scriptures and Religious Philosophy*.

Joseph Fielding Smith, one of the staunchest of the Brighamite theologians says:

> The Bible[14] teaches us that man existed in the spirit creation before he appeared on this earth with his physical body, but this doctrine in the Bible is only discerned through a mist or fog. This fog is created, as recorded by Nephi because many plain and precious things have been taken out of the Bible. . . . The doctrine of man's pre-existence in the spirit creation is clearly and forcefully taught.[15]
>
> The Latter-day Saints believe that man is a spirit clothed with a tabernacle the intelligent part of which was never created or made, but existed eternally. This belief is based upon a revelation given to the Church May 6, 1833, at Kirtland, Ohio.[16]

The revelation in question reads:

> Man also was in the beginning with God. Intelligence, or the light of truth, was not created or made neither indeed can be. . . . For man is spirit. The elements are eternal, and spirit and element, inseparably connected, received a fullness of joy.[17]

[14] Here Joseph Fielding Smith refers to the Bible as rewritten by Joseph Smith, specific quote, "Moses" 3:5-7. Readers of Mormon literature should always check Biblical references for accuracy.

[15] Joseph Fielding Smith, *The Progress of Man*, pp. 9-10.

[16] *Ibid.*, p. 11.

[17] *Doctrines and Covenants*, 93:29, 33, 34.

Joseph Fielding Smith, writing in a letter to Elder Whitney says:

> Our knowledge of persons and things before we came here, combined with the divinity awakened within our souls through obedience to the gospel . . . guides our preferences in the course of this life. . . . Can we know anything here that we did not know before we came? . . . I believe that our saviour possessed a foreknowledge of all of the vicissitudes through which he would pass in the mortal tabernacle. If Christ knew beforehand, so did we. But in coming here we forget all that our agency might be free indeed to choose good or evil.[18]

James E. Talmage, in explaining the transition from the previous state of man, states:

> It has been shown that mortality is divinely provided as a means of schooling and test, whereby the spirit offspring of God may develop their powers and demonstrate their characters. Every one of us has been advanced from the unembodied or pre-existent state to our present condition, in which the individual spirit is temporarily united with a body of flesh and bones.[19]

Later in this same chapter, Talmage refers to Jesus Christ as "the first born among all the spirit

[18] *Era*, 23:101; *Gospel Doctrine*, pp. 15-16.
[19] Talmage, *The Vitality of Mormonism*, pp. 48-49.

children of God," who "was to come to earth . . . to teach men the saving principles of the eternal Gospel."[20]

To Mormons the Fall was a fortuitous episode—distressing no doubt at the time to the participants—but absolutely necessary for the final advancement of men.

Regarding the Fall, Talmage writes:

> Through partaking of food unsuited to their condition and against which they had been specifically forewarned, the man and his wife became subject to physical degeneracy.[21]

Probably one of the most concise and yet comprehensive statements regarding man, his origin and destiny, according to Mormon doctrine, has been stated by John A. Widtsoe. We quote:

> He [man] existed before he came to earth; he was with God in the beginning; he accepted the opportunity provided by his father to come on earth to be tried, refined and educated; he lives on earth under laws and regulations and the authority of the Lord: he shall die, but in time he shall regain his body, and because of his righteous endeavors shall go on forever into eternal, active, progressive exhaltation. Man's destiny is divine. Life on earth is but a chapter in an eternal journey.

20 *Ibid.*, pp. 49-50.
21 *Ibid.*, p. 52.

Man is an eternal being. He also is "from everlasting to everlasting."

In this manner of thinking, salvation acquires a definite meaning. Whoever is in process of development or progression is in process of salvation. Increasing knowledge, used in conformity with the plan of the Lord, becomes power to remove all obstacles to progress. In the words of Joseph Smith, to be saved is to be placed "beyond the power of evil."

Clearly then, our salvation begun in the dim past, is being worked out by us on earth and will be approached in its greater perfection throughout the endless ages of future life. By this token all men may be saved but in degrees proportionate to their righteous works.

Does a man then save himself? From one point of view, yes. However, it is only through the divine plan that salvation may be won; therefore, man is only a partner in the saving process. Salvation is a co-operative enterprise between God and man.[22]

Contrast the complicated God-man theories with a simple statement of Scripture:

The Lord God formed man of the dust of the ground, and breathed into his nostrils the breath of life; and man became a living soul.[23]

22 John A. Widtsoe, Mormon section, *Varieties of American Religion*, pp. 132-133.

23 Genesis 2:7.

CHAPTER SEVEN

THE MORMONS AND SALVATION

SALVATION is a purely hypothetical proposition to the Mormon theologian. Since God is no more than an exalted man who passed through the experiences of an earthly existence, as do all men, there is no need for attaching to Him the attributes of absolute holiness and righteousness.

Since Jesus Christ is just another of God's children, even as we are, He loses His character as God the Son. There remains nothing unique about His Person and work.

Since man is not a sinner by nature, and since his sins can be nullified by water baptism at the age of eight, there is no great reason to worry about sin which carries no particular penalty. Unfortunately for the Mormons, the sin question cannot be shrugged off so lightly.

Joseph Smith's attitude toward sin and salvation is well expressed by Werner who says:

> In his youth, Joseph Smith was torn between the fear of not being saved eternally and the desire to have a good time from day to day. Fortunately for his peace of mind he was able to reconcile the two by having himself appointed by God to have a good time.[1]

Salvation in the Mormon philosophy is merely the preparation, by means of personal advancement in this life, for an expanded physical life in the next that does not carry with it the harassments of this life.

There is scarcely a shade of difference between the Mormon and the Moslem philosophies except that the Mormon scheme is the more highly developed and in keeping with experiences thought desirable by Occidentals, whereas the Moslem "Paradise" is based on Oriental values.

A fabulous new temple was completed in 1956 in Los Angeles. It is probably the most spectacular contemporary religious edifice in existence. This temple was open for inspection by the Gentiles for a period of weeks. It is now open only to Mormons in good standing for ritualistic purposes such as the sealing of marriages for eternity and baptism by proxy for the dead.

One of the features of the temple is a series of five rooms, the decor and murals of which depict the

[1] Morris Robert Werner, *Brigham Young, A Biography*, p. 63.

several stages of man's earthly history from Creation to his final state in a restored earthly paradise.

This final "celestial" room is intended to suggest the delights to be enjoyed by those who attain the celestial kingdom. *Time* Magazine describes it as "a luxurious sitting room with well-upholstered chairs and settees, delicate murals and elaborate chandeliers."[2] It suggests all that would be pleasing to ease-loving Americans who would like to live on and on in a physical body without physical ills or cares.

The American Indian had much the same philosophy, except that his idea of Heaven was a happy hunting ground where game was always available and where the wolf didn't stalk nor the north winds blow.

The Mormon paradise suggests nothing of the spiritual realm, and knows not the joy of unutterable peace of sins forgiven and a life compatible with the presence of God, to be enjoyed eternally in fellowship with the Father, the Son, the Holy Spirit and with the host of the redeemed.

In order to make a comparison of salvation as a Mormon sees it, and salvation as it is accepted by all orthodox Christians of whatever communion, we will state the Christian view of salvation and then quote from writers acceptable to the Mormons. The reader may come to his own conclusions. Salvation

[2] *Time*, January 16, 1956.

according to the Bible involves a threefold deliverance:

1. Deliverance from the penalty of sin, so that the sinner stands justified before God and cleansed from the guilt of sin. This guarantees him eternal life and eternal deliverance from judgment.

2. Deliverance from the power of sin in his daily life and throughout his earthly experience as a believer. This is made possible by the presence of the indwelling Spirit of God.

3. Deliverance, eventually, from the very presence of sin when the redeemed shall be ushered into the presence of God.

There are some slight variations, in the mode of expressing these three basic benefits of salvation, but all Christians will agree that these benefits are totally the results of the redemptive work of Christ on Calvary. Christians will agree that the work of Calvary was substitutionary. They believe that Jesus Christ, as man's Substitute, satisfied all of God's claims against fallen men with regard to sin. The validity of this redemptive work is assured by the physical resurrection of Jesus Christ from the dead, thus evidencing His triumph over death.

Salvation according to the Bible is available to all, regardless of the depth to which the sinner has descended in the quantity or quality of his sins, since the work of redemption at Calvary was complete. Salvation is attained by the acceptance of God's free gift as stated in Ephesians 2:8, 9: "By grace are ye saved through faith; and that not of yourselves: it is the gift of God: not of works, lest any man should boast."

Salvation is not attained by self-effort or good works. It does, however, give the believer the ability to produce good works, not for the purpose of perpetuating or enhancing his salvation, but because the yearning is present within the believer to produce fruit for God out of a sense of love for the Saviour.

Now, constrast this Christian and Biblical view of salvation with the Mormon view. It will be noticed that the Mormon writers borrow verses from the Bible to support their view but without discrimination as to the subject under discussion in the context of the Scripture used. Here is a statement by John A. Widtsoe who is considered by Mormons to be among their most competent apologists:

> What is salvation? It is the condition that results when a person is in harmony with truth. Man may ever be on the way to salvation, but in its fullness, salvation is the eternal goal. The law of salvation, as of all life, is eternal progression. One must grow daily and forever in righteousness and good works. Those who are in a state of salvation are in a constant state of progression. Those who are static or

who retrograde are "the lost." Even for the latter, the tender mercy of God provides a fitting place in His kingdom, and the opportunity for continuous repentance. Whoever has placed himself by obedience to divine law beyond the power of evil, to that extent is saved.

How may salvation be attained? By accepting the principles and practices of truth issuing from God and constituting the plan of salvation by the resolute use of the will to obey at any cost the requirements of the Gospel: and the constant appeal in prayer to God for assistance.

Does Christ do something for man which man cannot do for himself? Yes. He is our Redeemer; he leads us along the dim path; his sacrifice will enable us to recover the bodies we lay down in the grave; he is our advocate with the Father. He is our Captain.[3]

As to the antipathy manifested by Mormons toward the Christian view of salvation we quote an editorial from the church page of the *Deseret News,* which is the official daily newspaper of the Salt Lake Mormons.

A TWO-EDGED SWORD

Satan is the arch-deceiver. His doctrine appears under many a guise. Always he attempts to lead

[3] John A. Widtsoe, Mormon section, *Varieties of American Religion,* pp. 137-138.

people astray by holding before them false notions which on the surface seem much to be desired.

One of his most appealing methods of reaching mankind is to make them believe they can get something for nothing. Nearly everyone has enough selfishness to try to get all he can at the lowest price. Satan plays upon that trait. He does so in our economic life, and he does so in religion. Get something for nothing—or for as little as you can.

This identical philosophy is carried over into certain types of religion. Again it is to get something for nothing. Some teach that a person may have full salvation by whispering a few magic words. Just confess a belief in the Saviour—that is all. If you thus confess, you get full salvation, and nothing can keep you from it. No works are necessary, for you are saved by grace alone, so the teaching goes.

Get something—get salvation—for nothing but a phrase. Just say, "I believe." That is all there is to it, they declare. And they quote John 3:16 to support their arguments.

This unfounded fancy has become so popular with some that certain enthusiasts go to the extent of painting "John 3:16" on fences, on sign posts, on railroad overpasses, along the highways, anywhere. It is magic in their eyes, a magic way to be saved. But it is black magic, And they deceive themselves, for salvation comes not in that manner.

But is it not a striking thing that Satan would hold forth this same philosophy in both the fields of economics, or every-day bread-and-butter living, and in religion? And is it not remarkable that both these expressions of the same false philosophy are so popular with people?

The Lord has had a good deal to say about this matter, and his doctrine is just opposite to that of Lucifer. Instead of teaching us to get something for nothing, the Lord puts a premium upon production. His doctrine is that the idler shall not eat the bread nor wear the garments of the laborer.

And in religion it is the same. We are taught that we must work out our salvation. We must bring forth much fruit. Those branches of the vine which do not produce much good fruit shall be cut off and thrown into the fire. He emphasized production in his parable of the unprofitable servant. Faith without works is dead. On Judgment Day we shall be judged according to the deeds done in the body.

The Lord commands us to become perfect, even as he is. In giving us the commandment, and teaching us that we must work out our salvation, with prayer, and fasting, and increasing faith and testimony, he teaches us that we must put forth genuine effort for self-improvement.

How do we work out our salvation? By participating in the activities of the Church which develop in our souls those Christ-like traits that help

> us to become like him. That requires consistent, well-planned effort, with devotion to the end. So working out our salvation means developing Christ-like characters which will make us fit to come into the presence of the Lord.
>
> Latter-day Saints should not be deceived by Satan's philosophies of getting something for nothing. That false doctrine is like a two-edged sword which destroys either way it swings, whether in economics or in religion.[4]

It is quite obvious that the benefits of salvation, according to the Mormon philosophy, would be available only to a few very well-endowed persons. There is no provision for the derelict, the mediocre or the host of earth dwellers who would have no means or opportunity to produce the sort of effort prescribed by Mormon teachers.

By contrast the Christian message is to "whosoever will." The repentant sinner comes to Christ with words:

> Nothing in my hand I bring,
> Simply to Thy cross I cling.

The Mormon comes saying:

> Something in my hand I bring,
> To my own good works I cling.

Which will God accept?

[4] *Deseret News* (Salt Lake City, Utah: January 16, 1952).

CHAPTER EIGHT

THE MORMONS AND BAPTISM

One of Joseph Smith's excuses for not uniting with any of the Christian churches of his day was that they were not united in their views on baptism.

He was "stumbled" because the Presbyterians and Methodists sprinkled infants or grownups. The Baptists immersed only responsible believers. The Friends did not baptize at all. This was also the period in which Alexander Campbell was in the process of gathering a following. The Campbellites insisted that baptism by immersion was necessary for salvation.

Smith professed to have great distress over the subject, so since his new church was in process of being founded, it was to be expected that he would arrive at a decision regarding baptism. Smith relates that while he and Oliver Cowdry were translating the golden plates they came across mention of "baptism for the remission of sins."

Smith and Cowdry forthwith went into the woods to pray. Here they were met by a messenger from Heaven who turned out to be John the Baptist. He announced that he was about to confer upon them the priesthood of the Aaronic Order. Smith was ordered to baptize Cowdry and Cowdry in turn to baptize Smith. This accomplished, they were told that the Melchizedek priesthood would be conferred later by James, Peter, and John, who held this authority.[1] This occurred on May 15, 1829. By April, 1830, the *Book of Mormon* had been published and the new church organized.

By November of the same year the Church had acquired a theologian in the person of Sidney Rigdon. Rigdon was originally a Baptist who later followed Alexander Campbell and adopted his views on baptismal regeneration. He broke with Campbell when the latter failed to adopt Rigdon's ideas of communal living. Rigdon had established a following at Kirtland, Ohio, where the principle of holding all things in common was practiced. Rigdon's new church, apart from this communistic feature, followed closely the teaching of Campbell. The break came in August, 1830.

There is a gap in the record of Rigdon's activities

[1] *Pearl of Great Price*, p. 97.

during the next few months. One incident during this period was the conversion of Parley Pratt under the teaching of Rigdon. Within three weeks of his conversion he traveled east to New York State as an evangelist where he was reconverted to Mormonism under the preaching of Hyrum Smith, Joseph's brother.

Oliver Cowdry, Parley Pratt, and two companions were sent west by Smith to sell the *Book of Mormon* and to preach to the Indians. In a matter of days they visited Rigdon in Mentor, Ohio, and presented him with a *Book of Mormon*. Within two weeks (mid-November, 1830) Rigdon and his entire communal colony had accepted Mormonism and were baptized by Cowdry.

There seems to be no doubt but that Joseph Smith's views on baptism were really those of Rigdon.

There is good evidence (if circumstantial) that Rigdon could have been in touch with Smith during a considerable part of the developmental period of the Church, as well as the period of the writing of the *Book of Mormon*.

The calendar of Rigdon's life shows no entry for two months between June and August, 1828, nor for the weeks between October 13, 1828, and January 1, 1829. It was during this period that the manuscript of the *Book of Mormon* was progressing rapidly.

There is a gap from May until July, 1829. It was

during this interval that Smith and Cowdry baptized each other on the instructions of John the Baptist. We have noted elsewhere that Oliver Cowdry later commented on the fact that the voice of John the Baptist sounded amazingly like that of Elder Rigdon. It probably was Rigdon.[2]

It was during one of these absences of Rigdon from his home that one of the most important sections of the *Doctrines and Covenants* was prepared. This is Section 20 which bears the date of April, 1830. This section has complete instructions for the ordinance of baptism, the organization of the Church and the duties of its officers. This was not prepared by a novice but by one who knew all of the practices of the Church of that day. It parallels in most of its details the polity of the early Campbellite churches with which Rigdon was familiar and in which he was a leader.

It has too much Biblical content to have been written by Smith or Cowdry unaided. Smith, by the admission of his own family, was almost totally ignorant of the Bible in that period of his life.[3]

The story of Rigdon's conversion to Mormonism, as given by the Mormons, is that he accepted the *Book of Mormon* with gladness the first time it was presented to him and without having had oppor-

[2] Oliver Cowdry, *Defense*.
[3] Lucy Mack Smith, *Memoirs*.

tunity to give it more than a cursory examination. The "Gentile" version of the story is that Rigdon had been in contact with Smith during the period of the writing of the *Book of Mormon*. Some insist that it was he who made Solomon Spalding's *Manuscript Found* available to Smith.

Practically all of Smith's pronouncements were given in the form of "revelations." This is true even in the directives on purely mundane matters. There are abundant references to baptism and baptismal regeneration in all of his writings. The *Book of Mormon* contains thirty-two references to baptism. In one such reference, I Nephi 10:7-10, Lehi, a Jew living in Jerusalem in 600 B.C., prophesies in King James Version phraseology the exact sequence of the baptism of the Saviour by John the Baptist as related in the Gospels. The references to baptism increase in volume toward the latter part of the *Book of Mormon*. It is in these that the typical Rigdonian doctrines develop.

The most amazing reference, however, and the earliest in time sequence (although not revealed until at least five years after the completion of the *Book of Mormon*) is an elaborate record of the baptism by immersion of Adam! I quote at considerable length this amazing disclosure:

> God . . . called unto Adam . . . saying . . . if

thou wilt turn unto me . . . and believe and repent of all thy transgressions, and be baptized, even in water, in the name of mine only Begotten Son, who is full of grace and truth, which is Jesus Christ . . . ye shall receive the gift of the Holy Ghost.

And our father Adam spake unto the Lord and said: Why is it that men must repent and be baptized in water? And the Lord said unto Adam: Behold I have forgiven thee thy transgression in the Garden of Eden.

And now behold I say unto you: This is the plan of salvation unto all men, through the blood of mine only Begotten, who shall come to you in the meridian of time.

And it came to pass when the Lord had spoken unto Adam, our father, that Adam cried unto the Lord, and he was caught away by the Spirit of the Lord, and was carried into the water, and was laid under the water, and was brought forth out of the water.

And thus he was baptized and the spirit of God descended upon him, and thus he was born of the spirit, and became quickened in the inner man.

And he heard a voice out of heaven, saying: Thou art baptized with fire, and with the Holy Ghost.[4]

There are thirty-eight references to baptism in the

[4] *Pearl of Great Price,* Moses 6:51-54, 62, 65.

Doctrines and Covenants, one of which establishes the age at which the ordinance shall be administered:

> And their children shall be baptized for the remission of their sins when eight years old, and receive the laying on of hands.[5]

It will be agreed by all Mormon theologians that they teach unreservedly that there is no salvation in any age—past, present, or future—apart from water baptism. They do not even exempt from this law the thief on the cross who was told that he would be with the Saviour that day in Paradise.

They insist that the remission of sins is gained by the administration of baptism by an authorized person, and in this act the Holy Spirit is administered to the candidate. This is the total formula in connection with the "acceptance of the candidate into the Kingdom of God." In all of this they are forced to the admission that they consider the formula of baptism for the remission of sins to be the process by which salvation is initiated.

This is completely at variance with Biblical teaching. Baptism for the remission of sins and salvation from the penalty of sin are completely different propositions. An examination of the meaning of the term and its various usages in the New Testament will demonstrate this. The word for "remission" in

[5] *Doctrines and Covenants,* 68:27.

Greek is *aphesis*. It can be, and is, translated by the English words, *freedom, deliverance, forgiveness, liberty*, or the expressions, *to send away, to lay aside, to remit, to omit, to put away*. In classical Greek it is used for such situations as *dismissing a freed slave, exempting from obligation, to pass by*, or *to ignore*.

Regarding *remission of sins*, the term is used in the New Testament in two sequences in connection with baptism. The first of these relates to the baptism of John.[6] This was not a case of baptism following individual conversion, but rather of mass national repentance in preparation for the coming of the Messiah. This was not Christian baptism.

The second instance is in Acts 2:38 concerning the repentant Jews at Pentecost. This passage has caused a great deal of confusion regarding the relation between repentance and baptism. The famous Greek scholar A. T. Robertson explains how the problem is easily resolved in the Greek text. It should read: "You [plural] repent and let each one of you [singular] be baptized." "This change marks a break in the thought here that the English translation does not preserve. The first thing to do is make a radical and complete change of heart and life. Then let each one be baptized after this change

[6] Mark 1:4; Luke 3:3.

has taken place, and the act of baptism be performed 'in the name of Jesus Christ.'"[7]

We find that *remission of sins* is more often discussed apart from baptism than with it. Hebrews 9:22 tells us that "without shedding of blood is no remission [forgiveness]." This thought is also presented in Matthew 26:28 at the institution of the Lord's Supper. The Saviour says: "This is my blood of the new testament [covenant], which is shed for many for the remission of sins." While baptism is a symbol of the cleansing away of sins, only the "blood of Christ" applied to the sinner can make provision for the remission of sins.

When Peter was preaching to the household of Cornelius he said: "Whosoever believeth in him shall receive remission of sins."[8] Here remission of sins depends simply on accepting the Saviour by faith.

There is no contradiction in the three propositions. (1) The blood of Christ makes remission of sins possible; (2) Belief in the Lord Jesus makes it available; and (3) Baptism in the name of the Lord Jesus makes a demonstration of it.

The Greek word for "remission" is *aphesis* and is used in a number of connections in the New

[7] A. T. Robertson, *Word Pictures in the New Testament*, III, pp. 34-35.

[8] Acts 10:43.

Testament. It is used, for instance, in the Lord's prayer as *forgive*. Matthew 6:12-15 reads: "Forgive us our debts, as we forgive our debtors" or "remit our debts." In Matthew 18:21 Peter asks the Saviour, "How oft shall my brother sin against me, and I forgive him? Till seven times?" The Lord replies: "I say not . . . Until seven times: but, Until seventy times seven." The word *forgive* or *remit* here obviously has to do with the dismissal of our brother's offense from our mind and from the record. It has no connection with the cleansing of the sin in God's sight. This is something that must be effected between God and the individual, and is on the basis of the cleansing of sin by means of Calvary. This is developed in John's first epistle.

The Mormons pursue their argument for salvation by baptism by insisting that certain other Scriptures refer to water baptism. They insist, for instance, that when Paul writes concerning the Church to the Ephesians "that he might . . . cleanse it with the washing of water by the word,"[9] that he is speaking of water baptism.

One of the critical passages is John 3:5: "Except a man be born of water and of the Spirit, he cannot enter into the kingdom of God." There are two common interpretations of this passage: (1) The water refers to the cleansing effect of the Word of

[9] Ephesians 5:26.

God; (2) The water is a representation of the Spirit, *e.g.*, "born of water, *even* the Spirit." The latter view is possible from the Greek text and John 7:37-39 lends additional support. Whichever of these views is held, John 3:16 clearly states that faith alone secures salvation. This negates the efficaciousness of water baptism for obtaining eternal life.

In Titus 3:5 the Mormons take "washing of regeneration" to mean ceremonial water baptism, necessary for salvation. This *is* a reference to baptism, but it is the baptism of the Spirit whereby He places the believer into the body of Christ at the moment of belief. This is made clear in Romans 6:3-6 where baptism "is the picture or symbol of the new birth, not the means of securing it." [10]

The Mormons lay much stress on the authority of their priests to baptize for the remission of sins. They insist that only they, in this era, have the authority and that this authority was given them on May 15, 1829, by John the Baptist. Let us look at the record. On that significant occasion Joseph Smith and Oliver Cowdry were instructed to baptize each other. The messenger identified himself as John the Baptist.

Here are some problems. According to Scripture, the resurrection has not yet taken place, thus John the Baptist is still in the grave. There is no evidence

[10] Robertson, *op. cit.*, IV, p. 607.

that he re-appeared as Smith claimed, as a resurrected and glorified man. John the Baptist was never given any authority to ordain anyone or confer any priesthood. This is the sole province of the Head of the Church, Jesus Christ, yet Smith claims that John ordained him as an Aaronic priest at his baptism.

Whoever it was that appeared to Smith and Cowdry, if anyone did, was obviously an impostor. Furthermore, Joseph Smith was baptized by Oliver Cowdry, who soon became an apostate according to Smith's own testimony. Joseph Smith's authority is thus seen to be based on an unbiblical proposition, administered by an apostate, on the instructions of an impostor.

CHAPTER NINE

THE MORMONS AND BAPTISM FOR THE DEAD

THE MORMONS INSIST that there is no salvation except by water baptism administered by a qualified Mormon priest. They extend this teaching to include all of the millions who have lived and died on the earth without a knowledge of the "restored gospel" as it was revealed to Joseph Smith.

This reasoning could only result, sooner or later, in the formulation of a doctrine of baptism for the dead. Apparently the doctrine was first declared in 1841[1] when it was first mentioned in exact terms, although later teachers associate it with the appearance of Elijah to Joseph Smith and Oliver Cowdry in Kirtland, Ohio, on April 3, 1836.[2] Milton R. Hunter comments on these circumstances:

> "A week following the dedication of the Kirtland temple, April 3, 1836, Elijah appeared to

[1] *Doctrines and Covenants*, Sec. 128.
[2] *Ibid.*, Sec. 110.

> Joseph Smith and Oliver Cowdry in the temple and bestowed upon them the keys of sealing power, that all the ordinances for the dead might be performed in a valid way."[3]

Apparently the doctrine was not formulated during the Kirtland days since there is no record of baptisms having been performed for the dead until the installation of the baptismal font in the partially completed temple in Nauvoo, Ill. After the death of Smith and the departure of the "saints" from Nauvoo, the practice was not resumed until the erection of the temple in Salt Lake City.

The Mormon teachers, of course, insist that baptism for the dead was always practiced by the true church and that the true church, as it was restored by Joseph Smith, existed from the time of Adam. Smith, writing to the church in Sept. 6, 1842, speaks of the rite as follows:

> "—the ordinance that the Lord ordained and prepared before the foundation of the world, for the salvation of the dead who should die without a knowledge of the gospel."[4]

In the same revelation Joseph insists that the books referred to in Revelation 20:12, which will be opened at the judgment of the great white throne, are the

[3] Milton R. Hunter: *Gospel Through the Ages*, p. 224.
[4] *Doctrines and Covenants*, Sec. 128:5.

records of baptisms, and other rites, maintained by the official secretaries in connection with the "temple work."[5]

Milton Hunter, writing in his *Gospel Through the Ages,* which is one of the current texts for the instruction of the Melchizedek priesthood, brings Joseph Smith's teachings up to date. He says:

> "God not only revealed the doctrine of baptism for the living to the Prophet Joseph Smith but He established on earth again the glorious doctrine of baptism for the dead, thereby opening the door to all of His sons and daughters who have ever lived in mortality to come back into His presence on condition of their worthiness. The Lord told Joseph that baptism for the dead should be performed in His holy house; in fact, one of the principle purposes He had in mind in commanding the Latter-day Saints to build temples was for the performance of the holy ordinance. In the revelation the Lord declared: 'For a baptismal font there is not upon the earth, that they, my saints, may be baptized for those who are dead.'[6]
>
> "Then God commanded the saints to build temples in which to perform the ordinance of baptizing for the dead, proclaiming that this ordinance was instituted before the foundation of the world for the

[5] *Ibid.,* Sec. 128:6-9.
[6] *Ibid.,* 124:29-39.

salvation of His children who, for various reasons, would not accept the Gospel while in mortality."[7]

That none are exempt from this ordinance is made clear by James Talmage who cites the case of the repentant malefactor who was crucified with the Lord Jesus. Talmage says:

"To infer that the crucified transgressor was saved by his dying confession, and was granted a special passport to Heaven with sins unexpiated and without his compliance with the 'laws and ordinances of the Gospel' is to disregard both letter and spirit of scripture, and to ignore both reason and the sense of justice—the blessing promised him was to the effect that he should that day hear the gospel preached in Paradise.[8] In the acceptance or rejection of the message of salvation he would be left an agent to himself. The requirement of obedience to 'the laws and ordinances of the Gospel' was not waived, suspended or superseded in his case nor shall it be for any soul."[9]

The doctrine is defended as being scriptural by using Paul's reference to the practice:

What shall they do which are baptized for the

[7] Hunter: *Gospel Through the Ages*, pp. 223, 224.

[8] Mormons teach that Jesus preached the gospel to all of the dead during the three days between His death and resurrection. The repentant ones of these dead must then be baptized by living proxies. They use I Peter 3:19 as their proof text.

[9] Talmage: *Vitality of Mormonism*, pp. 70-71.

> dead, if the dead rise not at all? Why are they then baptized for the dead?[10]

Paul was not here discussing the subject of baptism or salvation but of the resurrection. Baptism for the dead was practiced only by heretical sects such as the Marcionites and Montanists, and was forbidden in A.D. 393 by the Council of Hippo. Regarding Paul's statement, A. F. Plummer states:

> The reference is clearly to something abnormal. There was some baptismal rite known to the Corinthians which would be meaningless without a belief in the resurrection. The passage does not imply that Saint Paul approves of the abnormal rite, but simply that it exists and implies the doctrine of the resurrection.[11]

Mormons are constantly doing "work for the dead" by compiling genealogies of their ancestors and other notables and then being baptized for them. The Mormons are very serious about all of this. One Mormon admitted to me that he had been baptized over five thousand times for the dead.

This is without doubt the most widespread activity of the Mormon church and is one of the chief purposes of the magnificent new temple in Los Angeles. Mormons claim that this temple has been built to

[10] I Corinthians 15:29.
[11] Hasting's *Dictionary of the Bible*, p. 245.

last throughout the Millennium and that during the thousand-year period, they will proceed to baptize, by proxy, all of the dead of the past ages who have not had a chance to respond to Smith's "restored gospel."

It would require the most highly developed computing device to calculate the total number of those in all of the ages of mankind's history who have never even heard of Joseph Smith. Also we predict that the total would be too stupendous to be accommodated by a thousand Mormon temples such as the one in Los Angeles.

One searches the scriptures in vain for any suggestion that those who have died out of Christ are to receive a second chance for salvation. Scripture is definite as to the fate of those who have rejected the Saviour. We read:

> "It is appointed unto men once to die but after this the judgment" (Heb. 9:27).

> "I saw the dead, small and great, stand before God; and the books were opened: and another book was opened, which is the book of life. . . . And whosoever was not found written in the book of life was cast into the lake of fire" (Rev. 20:12-15).

No greater authority can be quoted than the Lord Jesus as He tells, with His own lips, the story of the rich man and Lazarus. He describes with vivid detail the fixity of the condition of those in death. Read carefully Luke 16:19-31.

One also searches in vain for any scripture that would indicate that man is to be saved by his own good works, or the works of others performed in his behalf. We do read, however:

> "To him that worketh not, but believeth on him that justifieth the ungodly, his faith is counted for righteousness" (Rom. 4:5).
>
> "By grace are ye saved through faith; and that not of yourselves: it is the gift of God: not of works lest any man should boast" (Eph. 2:8-9).

For the benefit of any Mormon who reads these pages we discover that these verses, which we have just quoted, are rendered exactly as we have quoted them in Joseph Smith's *Inspired Version* of the Bible.

CONCLUSION

MANY CHRISTIANS, uninformed as to the true nature of the Mormon teachings, will defend their Mormon neighbors as good, clean-living, pious, honest folks. They will point to the wonderful relief practices of the Mormon Church. They will extol the thrift and industry of the Mormons as a whole. All of these things we recognize and appreciate as valuable contributions to society. We do not criticize these things.

But these virtues do not make one a Christian. Satan is delighted when his followers put up a good appearance. We insist that these virtues have nothing to do with one's acceptance before God if that one has never yielded to God's claims concerning His Son, Jesus Christ.

When Christians fail to demonstrate the above virtues, they are coming short of God's purpose, but these are the by-products of the Christian life.

In evaluating any religion, whether it is attractive or not, ask the following questions:

1. Does it accept God's Word, as it stands, without the addition of helps or explanations or additional "scripture"?
2. Does it, freely and unreservedly, give to the Lord Jesus His true place as the eternal Son of God?
3. Does it acknowledge His death as the only means whereby sinners may be saved?
4. Does it acknowledge man as a sinner, totally incompetent to save himself by his own merits?
5. Does it offer free salvation to anyone who comes to God? The ignorant, the vile, the derelict, the disturbed one?
6. Is it capable of making a saint out of a passion-ridden moral leper?
7. Is it the sort of faith that represents God reaching down in grace to man instead of showing man climbing upward on ladders of his own erection?

If it does not, it is not Christian. From such turn away.

BIBLIOGRAPHY

The Writings of Joseph Smith, Jr.

Book of Mormon: Palmyra, New York, Egbert B. Grandin: 1830.

Book of Mormon: Salt Lake edition of 1920.

Doctrines and Covenants of the Church of Jesus Christ of Latter-day Saints, carefully selected from the Revelations of God, and compiled by Joseph Smith, Jr., Oliver Cowdry, Sidney Rigdon. Quotations from Salt Lake edition of 1921. It differs somewhat from the collection used by the Reorganized Church.

The Holy Scriptures, translated and corrected by the spirit of Revelation. Known as the *Inspired Version.* Reorganized Church of Jesus Christ of Latter-day Saints, Plano, Illinois, 1867.

Pearl of Great Price, a choice selection from the revelations, translations, and narratives of Joseph Smith. Liverpool, 1909.

King Follett Discourse: with notes and references by the late Elder B. H. Roberts of the first Council of the

Seventy. Salt Lake City: Magazine Printing Company, 1955.

Mormon Periodicals and Newspapers Quoted

Handbook of Reference: Published at Kirtland, Ohio, 1835.

The Latter-day Saints *Millennial Star:* Liverpool, England, 1840 to present.

The Seer: A publication founded by Orson Pratt in honor of Joseph Smith, Jr.

Salt Lake Tribune: Issue of August 15, 1909.

Salt Lake Herald: Issue of November 6, 1898.

The Deseret News: Issue of January 16, 1952.

Time Magazine: Issue of January 16, 1956.

Books and Pamphlets

BARKER, JAMES L. *The Divine Church:* A course of study for the Melchizedek priesthood. Quorums for the year 1952. Deseret News Publishers.

BRODIE, FAWN MCKAY. *No Man Knows My History.* The Life of Joseph Smith. New York: Alfred Knopf, 1945.

CHAFER, LEWIS SPERRY. *Systematic Theology.* Dallas, Texas: The Dallas Theological Seminary, 1947.

COWDRY, OLIVER. *Defense* in a rehearsal of my grounds for separating myself from the Latter-day Saints. Norton, Ohio: Pressley's Job Shop, 1839.

CURTIS, BARDELLA SHIPP. *Sacred Scriptures and Religious Philosophy.* Caldwell, Idaho: Caxton Printers, 1922.

HASTINGS, THOMAS. *Dictionary of the Bible.*

EVANS, JOHN HENRY. *An American Prophet.* New York: Macmillan and Co., 1933.

HUNTER, MILTON R. *The Gospel Through the Ages.* Salt Lake City: Steven and Wallis Publishing Co.

JACQUES, JOHN. *A Catechism of Mormon Doctrine.*

Journal of Discourses. A collection of Sermons by Brigham Young, Orson Pratt, Heber Kimball and others, 1854 to 1886, Salt Lake City. The "others" include Parley Pratt and Orson Hyde, both of whom are quoted.

PRATT, ORSON. *Absurdities of Materialism.* Salt Lake City.

PRATT, PARLEY P. *Key to the Science of Theology.* An Introduction to the First Principles of Spiritual Philosophy. Salt Lake City: George Q. Cannon and Sons, 1891.

SMITH, JOSEPH FIELDING. *The Progress of Man.* Genealogical Society of Utah, Deseret News Press, 1936.

SMITH, LUCY MACK. *Memoirs.* Biographical sketches of Joseph Smith the Prophet and his progenitors for many generations, Liverpool, 1953. (Banned by Brigham Young: Current editions completely revised from the original editions.)

SPALDING, BISHOP, F. S. *Joseph Smith, Jr., as a Translator.* Salt Lake: 1912. Department of Missions: Reformed Episcopal Church.

TALMAGE, JAMES E. *The Articles of Faith.* An Exposition of the Doctrinal Statement of the Latter-day Saints. Salt Lake: 1929.

———. *The Vitality of Mormonism*. Boston: Richard G. Badger, publisher, 1919.

WERNER, MORRIS ROBERT. *Brigham Young, A Biography*. New York: Harcourt Brace and Co., 1925.

WIDTSOE, JOHN A., PH.D. Mormon Section of *Varieties of American Religion* ed. Charles Samuel Braden, Ph.D., Chicago: Willett, Clark and Co., 1936.